50 Low-Carb Asian Noodle Bowls Recipes for Home

By: Kelly Johnson

Table of Contents

- Zucchini Pad Thai
- Shirataki Sesame Ginger Noodles
- Spaghetti Squash Teriyaki Bowls
- Cauliflower Fried Rice Noodle Bowl
- Kelp Noodle Kimchi Stir-Fry
- Daikon Radish Pho
- Cabbage Pad See Ew
- Tofu Shirataki Ramen
- Broccoli and Beef Shirataki Noodles
- Thai Basil Chicken Cucumber Noodles
- Low-Carb Japchae with Beef
- Cabbage and Carrot Soba Noodle Stir-Fry
- Coconut Curry Shirataki Noodles
- Spiralized Cucumber and Shrimp Salad
- Almond Butter Thai Noodle Bowl
- Keto-friendly Miso Soup with Tofu Shirataki
- Sesame Almond Zoodle Bowl
- Shirataki Noodle Tom Yum Soup
- Jicama Pad Thai Salad
- Low-Carb Bibimbap Bowl
- Egg Drop Shirataki Soup
- Kelp Noodle Coconut Curry Bowl
- Cabbage and Broccoli Lo Mein
- Peanut Zoodle Stir-Fry
- Cucumber Soba Noodle Salad
- Tofu Shirataki Pad Kee Mao
- Keto Teriyaki Chicken Konjac Noodles
- Lemongrass Chicken Shirataki Bowl
- Radish Noodle Kimchi Bibim Guksu
- Thai Basil Zoodle Bowl
- Low-Carb Ramen with Chicken and Bok Choy
- Cabbage Pad Thai Salad
- Spaghetti Squash Bulgogi Bowl
- Keto-friendly Pho with Kelp Noodles
- Shirataki Noodle Teriyaki Salmon Bowl

- Sesame Ginger Cabbage Noodles
- Almond Butter Chicken Zoodle Stir-Fry
- Jicama Noodle Spring Roll Bowl
- Spiralized Daikon Radish Yakisoba
- Cauliflower Kimchi Fried Rice Bowl
- Zoodle Tom Kha Gai Soup
- Cabbage and Shrimp Soba Noodle Stir-Fry
- Keto-friendly Laksa with Shirataki Noodles
- Thai Basil Beef and Cucumber Noodles
- Kelp Noodle Thai Coconut Soup
- Spiralized Zucchini and Chicken Satay Bowl
- Teriyaki Tofu Shirataki Noodle Bowl
- Cucumber and Radish Somen Salad
- Low-Carb Vietnamese Bun Thit Nuong Bowl
- Cauliflower Shrimp Pad See Ew

Zucchini Pad Thai

Ingredients:

- 2 large zucchinis, spiralized into noodles
- 1 cup cooked and diced chicken, shrimp, or tofu (protein of your choice)
- 2 eggs, beaten
- 1 cup bean sprouts
- 1/2 cup chopped green onions
- 1/4 cup chopped peanuts
- 2 tablespoons oil (sesame or vegetable oil)
- 3 cloves garlic, minced
- 1 tablespoon fresh ginger, grated
- 1/4 cup soy sauce or tamari (for gluten-free)
- 2 tablespoons fish sauce
- 1 tablespoon rice vinegar
- 1 tablespoon Sriracha sauce (adjust to taste)
- 1 tablespoon sugar substitute (like erythritol or monk fruit) - optional
- Lime wedges for serving

Instructions:

Prepare the Sauce:
    In a small bowl, mix together soy sauce, fish sauce, rice vinegar, Sriracha, and sugar substitute. Set aside.

Cook the Protein:
    In a large pan or wok, heat oil over medium-high heat. Add minced garlic and grated ginger, sauté for about 1 minute until fragrant. Add the cooked chicken, shrimp, or tofu, and cook until heated through.

Add Eggs:
    Push the protein to one side of the pan and pour the beaten eggs into the other side. Scramble the eggs until cooked, then mix them with the protein.

Add Zucchini Noodles:
    Add the spiralized zucchini noodles to the pan. Toss and cook for 2-3 minutes until they are just tender but still have a bit of crunch.

Combine Ingredients:
> Pour the prepared sauce over the noodles and toss everything together until well combined.

Add Vegetables:
> Stir in bean sprouts and chopped green onions. Cook for an additional 1-2 minutes.

Serve:
> Divide the Zucchini Pad Thai among plates. Top with chopped peanuts and serve with lime wedges on the side.

Enjoy this low-carb and flavorful Zucchini Pad Thai as a satisfying and healthy alternative to the classic dish!

Shirataki Sesame Ginger Noodles

Ingredients:

- 2 packs (about 400g) of shirataki noodles, drained and rinsed
- 1 cup thinly sliced vegetables (bell peppers, carrots, broccoli, etc.)
- 1/2 cup sliced mushrooms
- 1/4 cup soy sauce or tamari (for gluten-free)
- 2 tablespoons sesame oil
- 1 tablespoon rice vinegar
- 1 tablespoon fresh ginger, minced
- 2 cloves garlic, minced
- 1 tablespoon sesame seeds (for garnish)
- Green onions, chopped (for garnish)

Instructions:

Prepare the Shirataki Noodles:
Rinse the shirataki noodles thoroughly under cold water and drain them well. You may also want to boil them for 2-3 minutes to eliminate any residual odor.

Stir-Fry Vegetables:
Heat sesame oil in a large skillet or wok over medium-high heat. Add sliced vegetables and mushrooms. Stir-fry for 3-5 minutes until they are slightly tender but still crisp.

Prepare the Sauce:
In a small bowl, whisk together soy sauce, rice vinegar, minced ginger, and minced garlic.

Add Noodles:
Add the drained shirataki noodles to the pan with the vegetables. Toss them together, ensuring the noodles are well-coated with the oil and vegetables.

Pour Sauce Over Noodles:
Pour the sauce over the noodles and vegetables. Toss continuously for 2-3 minutes until everything is well combined and heated through.

Serve:

Divide the Shirataki Sesame Ginger Noodles among plates. Garnish with sesame seeds and chopped green onions.

Optional Additions:
You can add protein such as tofu, chicken, or shrimp for an extra boost.

Enjoy this light and flavorful dish that captures the essence of sesame and ginger without the carb-heavy noodles!

Spaghetti Squash Teriyaki Bowls

Ingredients:

For the Spaghetti Squash:

- 1 medium-sized spaghetti squash
- 2 tablespoons olive oil
- Salt and pepper to taste

For the Teriyaki Sauce:

- 1/2 cup soy sauce or tamari (for gluten-free)
- 3 tablespoons water
- 2 tablespoons rice vinegar
- 1 tablespoon sesame oil
- 2 tablespoons low-carb sweetener (like erythritol or monk fruit)
- 2 cloves garlic, minced
- 1 teaspoon fresh ginger, grated
- 1 tablespoon cornstarch (optional, for thickening)

Other Ingredients:

- 1 cup broccoli florets
- 1 cup sliced bell peppers (color of your choice)
- 1 cup snap peas, trimmed
- 1 cup sliced carrots
- 1 tablespoon sesame seeds (for garnish)
- Chopped green onions (for garnish)
- Cooked protein of your choice (chicken, beef, tofu, shrimp, etc.)

Instructions:

Prepare the Spaghetti Squash:
- Preheat the oven to 400°F (200°C).
- Cut the spaghetti squash in half lengthwise and scoop out the seeds.
- Drizzle the cut sides with olive oil and season with salt and pepper.
- Place the squash, cut side down, on a baking sheet and roast for 40-45 minutes or until the flesh is tender.

Scrape the Squash:

- Allow the spaghetti squash to cool slightly, then use a fork to scrape the flesh into spaghetti-like strands.

Prepare the Teriyaki Sauce:
- In a small saucepan, combine soy sauce, water, rice vinegar, sesame oil, low-carb sweetener, minced garlic, and grated ginger.
- If you prefer a thicker sauce, mix cornstarch with a little water to create a slurry. Add the slurry to the sauce mixture.
- Heat the sauce over medium heat, stirring continuously until it thickens. Remove from heat.

Stir-Fry Vegetables:
- In a large skillet or wok, stir-fry the broccoli, bell peppers, snap peas, and carrots until they are crisp-tender.

Combine Ingredients:
- Add the cooked spaghetti squash strands to the skillet along with the prepared teriyaki sauce. Toss everything together until well coated.

Add Protein:
- Stir in the cooked protein of your choice until it's heated through and coated with the teriyaki sauce.

Serve:
- Divide the Spaghetti Squash Teriyaki Bowls among plates. Garnish with sesame seeds and chopped green onions.

Enjoy these flavorful and satisfying teriyaki bowls with the goodness of spaghetti squash!

Cauliflower Fried Rice Noodle Bowl

Ingredients:

For the Cauliflower Fried Rice:

- 1 medium-sized cauliflower, grated or processed into rice-like texture
- 2 tablespoons oil (olive oil or sesame oil)
- 1 cup diced mixed vegetables (carrots, peas, corn, bell peppers, etc.)
- 2 cloves garlic, minced
- 1 tablespoon ginger, grated
- 2 eggs, beaten
- 3 tablespoons soy sauce or tamari (for gluten-free)
- 1 tablespoon oyster sauce (optional)
- Salt and pepper to taste
- Green onions, chopped (for garnish)

For the Noodle Bowl:

- Shirataki noodles or zucchini noodles (prepared according to package instructions)
- Cooked protein of your choice (chicken, shrimp, tofu, etc.)

Instructions:

Prepare Cauliflower Rice:
- Grate or process the cauliflower into rice-sized pieces.
- In a large skillet or wok, heat oil over medium-high heat. Add garlic and ginger, sauté for 1-2 minutes until fragrant.

Cook Vegetables:
- Add the diced mixed vegetables to the skillet. Stir-fry for 3-5 minutes until they are slightly tender but still crisp.

Add Cauliflower Rice:
- Add the cauliflower rice to the skillet. Stir-fry for an additional 5-7 minutes until the cauliflower is cooked but not mushy.

Create Well in the Center:
- Push the cauliflower rice and vegetables to the sides of the skillet, creating a well in the center.

Cook Eggs:

- Pour the beaten eggs into the center well. Allow them to cook for a minute or so, then scramble them until fully cooked.

Combine Ingredients:
- Mix the cooked eggs with the cauliflower rice and vegetables.

Season with Sauce:
- Pour soy sauce and oyster sauce over the mixture. Stir well to combine. Season with salt and pepper to taste.

Prepare Noodle Bowl:
- In a separate bowl, combine prepared shirataki or zucchini noodles with the cauliflower fried rice mixture.

Add Protein:
- Stir in your cooked protein of choice until heated through.

Serve:
- Divide the Cauliflower Fried Rice Noodle Bowl among plates. Garnish with chopped green onions.

Enjoy this flavorful and satisfying low-carb noodle bowl that's both nutritious and delicious!

Kelp Noodle Kimchi Stir-Fry

Ingredients:

- 2 packs (about 400g) of kelp noodles, rinsed and drained
- 1 cup kimchi, chopped
- 1 cup firm tofu, cubed
- 1 cup mixed vegetables (bell peppers, broccoli, carrots, etc.), sliced
- 2 tablespoons sesame oil
- 3 tablespoons soy sauce or tamari (for gluten-free)
- 1 tablespoon rice vinegar
- 1 tablespoon gochugaru (Korean red pepper flakes) - adjust to taste
- 1 tablespoon toasted sesame seeds (for garnish)
- Green onions, chopped (for garnish)

Instructions:

Prepare Kelp Noodles:
- Rinse the kelp noodles under cold water and drain them well. If the noodles are too long, you can cut them with kitchen scissors.

Stir-Fry Tofu:
- In a large skillet or wok, heat sesame oil over medium-high heat. Add cubed tofu and stir-fry until golden brown on all sides. Remove tofu from the skillet and set aside.

Stir-Fry Vegetables:
- In the same skillet, add more sesame oil if needed. Stir-fry the mixed vegetables until they are slightly tender but still crisp.

Add Kimchi:
- Add chopped kimchi to the vegetables in the skillet. Stir-fry for 2-3 minutes to incorporate the flavors.

Combine Kelp Noodles:
- Add the prepared kelp noodles to the skillet. Toss everything together until well combined.

Prepare Sauce:
- In a small bowl, mix soy sauce, rice vinegar, and gochugaru. Adjust the spiciness to your liking.

Pour Sauce Over Noodles:
- Pour the sauce over the kelp noodles and stir-fry mixture. Toss until the noodles are coated with the sauce.

Add Tofu:

- Add the stir-fried tofu back into the skillet. Toss everything together until heated through.

Serve:
- Divide the Kelp Noodle Kimchi Stir-Fry among plates. Garnish with toasted sesame seeds and chopped green onions.

Enjoy this flavorful and low-carb stir-fry that combines the umami of kimchi with the unique texture of kelp noodles!

Daikon Radish Pho

Ingredients:

For the Broth:

- 8 cups beef or vegetable broth
- 1 large onion, sliced
- 3-inch piece of ginger, sliced
- 3-4 star anise
- 3-4 cloves
- 1 cinnamon stick
- 1 tablespoon coriander seeds
- 1 tablespoon soy sauce or tamari (for gluten-free)
- 1 tablespoon fish sauce (adjust to taste)
- Salt and pepper to taste

For the Daikon Radish Noodles:

- 1 large daikon radish, peeled and spiralized into noodles
- 2 tablespoons oil (sesame or vegetable oil)
- Salt and pepper to taste

Toppings:

- Thinly sliced beef, cooked rare (optional)
- Bean sprouts
- Fresh basil leaves
- Lime wedges
- Thinly sliced green onions
- Red chili slices (optional)

Instructions:

Prepare the Broth:
- In a large pot, combine beef or vegetable broth, sliced onion, ginger, star anise, cloves, cinnamon stick, coriander seeds, soy sauce, and fish sauce.
- Bring the broth to a boil, then reduce the heat to low and simmer for at least 30-40 minutes to allow the flavors to meld.
- Season the broth with salt and pepper to taste. Strain the broth and discard the solids.

Prepare Daikon Radish Noodles:

- In a separate pan, heat oil over medium-high heat. Add daikon radish noodles and sauté for 5-7 minutes until they are slightly tender but still have a bite.
- Season with salt and pepper to taste.

Assemble Pho Bowls:
- Divide the daikon radish noodles among serving bowls.
- Pour the hot broth over the noodles.

Add Toppings:
- Add thinly sliced beef (if using), bean sprouts, fresh basil leaves, lime wedges, sliced green onions, and red chili slices.

Serve:
- Serve the Daikon Radish Pho hot, allowing each person to customize their bowl with toppings and condiments.

Enjoy this comforting and flavorful Daikon Radish Pho that provides the taste of traditional Vietnamese pho with a low-carb twist!

Cabbage Pad See Ew

Ingredients:

- 1 small head of cabbage, thinly sliced
- 2 tablespoons oil (vegetable or sesame oil)
- 2 cloves garlic, minced
- 1 cup protein of choice (thinly sliced chicken, beef, tofu, or shrimp)
- 2 eggs, beaten
- 2 tablespoons soy sauce or tamari (for gluten-free)
- 1 tablespoon oyster sauce
- 1 tablespoon fish sauce
- 1 tablespoon dark soy sauce (for color)
- 1 tablespoon sugar substitute (like erythritol or monk fruit)
- White pepper to taste
- Green onions, chopped (for garnish)

Instructions:

Prepare Cabbage:
- Thinly slice the cabbage into noodle-like strips.

Stir-Fry Protein:
- In a large wok or skillet, heat oil over medium-high heat. Add minced garlic and stir-fry for about 30 seconds until fragrant.
- Add the protein of your choice and cook until browned and cooked through.

Push Protein to One Side:
- Push the protein to one side of the wok, creating space for the eggs.

Scramble Eggs:
- Pour the beaten eggs into the empty side of the wok. Allow them to set slightly, then scramble them until fully cooked.

Combine Ingredients:
- Mix the scrambled eggs with the protein in the wok.

Add Cabbage:
- Add the thinly sliced cabbage to the wok. Stir-fry for 3-5 minutes until the cabbage is tender but still has a bit of crunch.

Prepare Sauce:
- In a small bowl, whisk together soy sauce, oyster sauce, fish sauce, dark soy sauce, sugar substitute, and white pepper.

Pour Sauce Over Cabbage:

- Pour the sauce over the cabbage and protein mixture. Toss everything together until well coated and heated through.

Adjust Seasoning:
- Taste and adjust the seasoning if needed. You can add more soy sauce, fish sauce, or sugar substitute according to your preferences.

Serve:
- Divide the Cabbage Pad See Ew among plates. Garnish with chopped green onions.

Enjoy this light and flavorful low-carb alternative to traditional Pad See Ew!

Tofu Shirataki Ramen

Ingredients:

For the Broth:

- 4 cups vegetable broth
- 2 cloves garlic, minced
- 1 tablespoon fresh ginger, grated
- 2 tablespoons low-sodium soy sauce or tamari (for gluten-free)
- 1 tablespoon sesame oil
- 1 tablespoon rice vinegar
- 1 teaspoon miso paste
- Salt and pepper to taste

For the Tofu Shirataki Noodles:

- 2 packs (about 400g) of tofu shirataki noodles, drained and rinsed
- 1 tablespoon oil (sesame or vegetable oil)
- 1 cup sliced mushrooms
- 1 cup baby spinach or bok choy
- 1/2 cup shredded carrots
- 1/2 cup sliced bamboo shoots
- 1/2 cup sliced green onions (for garnish)

Optional Toppings:

- Firm tofu, cubed and pan-fried
- Nori sheets, sliced
- Soft-boiled egg
- Chili oil or Sriracha (for extra heat)

Instructions:

Prepare Tofu Shirataki Noodles:
- Rinse the tofu shirataki noodles under cold water and drain them well. If desired, you can blanch them in hot water for a couple of minutes to remove any residual smell.

Stir-Fry Vegetables:

- In a large pot or wok, heat oil over medium-high heat. Add sliced mushrooms, shredded carrots, and bamboo shoots. Stir-fry for 3-5 minutes until they are slightly tender.

Prepare Broth:
- In the same pot, add minced garlic and grated ginger. Sauté for about 1 minute until fragrant.
- Pour in vegetable broth, soy sauce, sesame oil, rice vinegar, and miso paste. Bring the broth to a simmer and let it cook for 5-7 minutes to allow the flavors to meld. Season with salt and pepper to taste.

Add Tofu Shirataki Noodles:
- Add the prepared tofu shirataki noodles to the pot. Allow them to simmer in the broth for 2-3 minutes until heated through.

Stir in Greens:
- Add baby spinach or bok choy to the pot. Stir until the greens are wilted.

Adjust Seasoning:
- Taste the broth and adjust the seasoning if needed. You can add more soy sauce, sesame oil, or rice vinegar according to your preferences.

Serve:
- Ladle the Tofu Shirataki Ramen into bowls. Top with sliced green onions and any optional toppings you desire.

Enjoy this light and flavorful Tofu Shirataki Ramen as a satisfying low-carb alternative to traditional ramen!

Broccoli and Beef Shirataki Noodles

Ingredients:

For the Beef Marinade:

- 1/2 pound (about 225g) beef sirloin or flank steak, thinly sliced
- 2 tablespoons soy sauce or tamari (for gluten-free)
- 1 tablespoon oyster sauce
- 1 tablespoon sesame oil
- 1 teaspoon cornstarch

For the Stir-Fry:

- 2 packs (about 400g) shirataki noodles, drained and rinsed
- 2 tablespoons oil (vegetable or sesame oil)
- 2 cloves garlic, minced
- 1 tablespoon fresh ginger, grated
- 1 cup broccoli florets
- 1 red bell pepper, thinly sliced
- 1 carrot, julienned
- 2 tablespoons soy sauce or tamari
- 1 tablespoon oyster sauce
- 1 tablespoon hoisin sauce
- 1 tablespoon rice vinegar
- Sesame seeds and sliced green onions for garnish

Instructions:

Marinate the Beef:
- In a bowl, combine thinly sliced beef with soy sauce, oyster sauce, sesame oil, and cornstarch. Allow it to marinate for at least 15-20 minutes.

Prepare Shirataki Noodles:
- Rinse the shirataki noodles under cold water and drain well. You may want to blanch them in hot water for a couple of minutes to remove any residual odor.

Stir-Fry Beef:
- Heat oil in a large skillet or wok over medium-high heat. Add marinated beef and stir-fry for 2-3 minutes until browned. Remove the beef from the skillet and set aside.

Stir-Fry Vegetables:
- In the same skillet, add a bit more oil if needed. Sauté minced garlic and grated ginger for about 1 minute until fragrant.
- Add broccoli florets, red bell pepper, and julienned carrot. Stir-fry for 3-5 minutes until the vegetables are tender-crisp.

Combine Beef and Vegetables:
- Add the cooked beef back to the skillet with the vegetables. Mix well.

Add Shirataki Noodles:
- Add the drained shirataki noodles to the skillet. Toss everything together until well combined.

Prepare Sauce:
- In a small bowl, whisk together soy sauce, oyster sauce, hoisin sauce, and rice vinegar.

Pour Sauce Over Noodles:
- Pour the sauce over the noodles and stir-fry mixture. Toss until everything is coated and heated through.

Adjust Seasoning:
- Taste and adjust the seasoning if needed. You can add more soy sauce or other sauces according to your taste.

Serve:
- Divide the Broccoli and Beef Shirataki Noodles among plates. Garnish with sesame seeds and sliced green onions.

Enjoy this delicious and low-carb twist on the classic Beef and Broccoli stir-fry!

Thai Basil Chicken Cucumber Noodles

Ingredients:

For the Chicken Marinade:

- 1 pound (about 450g) boneless, skinless chicken breasts or thighs, thinly sliced
- 2 tablespoons soy sauce or tamari (for gluten-free)
- 1 tablespoon oyster sauce
- 1 tablespoon fish sauce
- 1 tablespoon sesame oil
- 1 teaspoon sugar substitute (like erythritol or monk fruit)

For the Cucumber Noodles:

- 4 large cucumbers, spiralized into noodles
- 1 tablespoon salt

For the Stir-Fry:

- 2 tablespoons oil (vegetable or coconut oil)
- 4 cloves garlic, minced
- 1-2 red chili peppers, sliced (adjust to taste)
- 1 bell pepper, thinly sliced
- 1 cup cherry tomatoes, halved
- 1 cup fresh basil leaves, torn

Optional Garnishes:

- Lime wedges
- Chopped peanuts
- Sliced green onions

Instructions:

    Marinate the Chicken:
- In a bowl, combine thinly sliced chicken with soy sauce, oyster sauce, fish sauce, sesame oil, and sugar substitute. Let it marinate for about 15-20 minutes.

    Prepare Cucumber Noodles:

- Spiralize the cucumbers into noodles. Place them in a colander, sprinkle with salt, and let them sit for 10-15 minutes to release excess water. Rinse and drain well.

Stir-Fry Chicken:
- Heat oil in a large skillet or wok over medium-high heat. Add minced garlic and sliced red chili peppers. Sauté for about 1 minute until fragrant.
- Add the marinated chicken to the skillet. Stir-fry for 5-7 minutes until the chicken is cooked through and slightly caramelized.

Add Vegetables:
- Add sliced bell pepper and cherry tomatoes to the skillet. Stir-fry for an additional 3-4 minutes until the vegetables are tender-crisp.

Combine Cucumber Noodles:
- Pat the cucumber noodles dry with paper towels. Add them to the skillet with the cooked chicken and vegetables. Toss everything together until well combined.

Finish with Basil:
- Add torn basil leaves to the skillet. Toss until the basil is wilted and evenly distributed.

Adjust Seasoning:
- Taste and adjust the seasoning if needed. You can add more soy sauce or fish sauce according to your taste.

Serve:
- Divide the Thai Basil Chicken Cucumber Noodles among plates. Garnish with lime wedges, chopped peanuts, and sliced green onions if desired.

Enjoy this light and flavorful Thai-inspired dish that's perfect for a quick and healthy meal!

Low-Carb Japchae with Beef

Ingredients:

For the Beef Marinade:

- 1/2 pound (about 225g) beef sirloin or ribeye, thinly sliced
- 2 tablespoons soy sauce or tamari (for gluten-free)
- 1 tablespoon sesame oil
- 1 tablespoon erythritol or monk fruit sweetener
- 1 teaspoon minced garlic
- 1 teaspoon grated ginger

For the Noodles and Vegetables:

- 2 packs (about 400g) of shirataki noodles, drained and rinsed
- 2 tablespoons oil (vegetable or sesame oil)
- 1 onion, thinly sliced
- 1 carrot, julienned
- 1 red bell pepper, thinly sliced
- 1 cup spinach, blanched and drained
- 2 green onions, sliced
- Sesame seeds for garnish

For the Sauce:

- 3 tablespoons soy sauce or tamari
- 1 tablespoon sesame oil
- 1 tablespoon erythritol or monk fruit sweetener
- 1 teaspoon minced garlic

Instructions:

Marinate the Beef:
- In a bowl, combine thinly sliced beef with soy sauce, sesame oil, sweetener, minced garlic, and grated ginger. Allow it to marinate for at least 15-20 minutes.

Prepare Shirataki Noodles:
- Rinse the shirataki noodles under cold water and drain them well. If desired, you can blanch them in hot water for a couple of minutes to remove any residual odor.

Stir-Fry Beef:

- Heat oil in a large skillet or wok over medium-high heat. Add the marinated beef and stir-fry for 2-3 minutes until browned. Remove the beef from the skillet and set aside.

Stir-Fry Vegetables:
- In the same skillet, add a bit more oil if needed. Sauté sliced onion, julienned carrot, and red bell pepper until the vegetables are tender-crisp.

Add Spinach and Green Onions:
- Add blanched spinach and sliced green onions to the skillet. Stir-fry for an additional 1-2 minutes.

Combine Noodles:
- Add the prepared shirataki noodles to the skillet. Toss everything together until well combined.

Prepare Sauce:
- In a small bowl, whisk together soy sauce, sesame oil, sweetener, and minced garlic.

Pour Sauce Over Noodles:
- Pour the sauce over the noodles and vegetables. Toss until everything is coated and heated through.

Add Beef:
- Add the stir-fried beef back to the skillet. Toss until it's evenly distributed throughout the dish.

Adjust Seasoning:
- Taste and adjust the seasoning if needed. You can add more soy sauce or sweetener according to your taste.

Serve:
- Divide the Low-Carb Japchae with Beef among plates. Garnish with sesame seeds.

Enjoy this flavorful and low-carb version of Japchae with all the deliciousness of the classic Korean dish!

Cabbage and Carrot Soba Noodle Stir-Fry

Ingredients:

For the Stir-Fry:

- 8 oz (about 225g) soba noodles
- 2 tablespoons oil (vegetable or sesame oil)
- 3 cups green cabbage, thinly sliced
- 1 cup carrots, julienned
- 1 bell pepper (color of your choice), thinly sliced
- 3 green onions, sliced
- 2 cloves garlic, minced
- 1 tablespoon fresh ginger, grated
- 1/4 cup soy sauce or tamari (for gluten-free)
- 1 tablespoon oyster sauce
- 1 tablespoon rice vinegar
- 1 tablespoon sesame seeds (for garnish)
- Lime wedges (for serving)

Optional Protein Additions:

- Tofu cubes
- Shrimp, chicken, or beef slices

Instructions:

Cook Soba Noodles:
- Cook soba noodles according to package instructions. Drain and rinse under cold water to stop the cooking process. Set aside.

Prepare Stir-Fry Sauce:
- In a small bowl, whisk together soy sauce, oyster sauce, and rice vinegar. Set aside.

Stir-Fry Vegetables:
- Heat oil in a large wok or skillet over medium-high heat. Add minced garlic and grated ginger, sauté for about 1 minute until fragrant.
- Add sliced cabbage, julienned carrots, bell pepper, and green onions to the wok. Stir-fry for 5-7 minutes until the vegetables are tender-crisp.

Optional Protein:

- If adding protein, push the vegetables to the side of the wok and cook the protein until browned and cooked through. Then, mix it with the vegetables.

Combine Noodles:
- Add the cooked soba noodles to the wok. Toss everything together until the noodles are well-coated with the vegetables.

Pour Sauce Over Noodles:
- Pour the prepared sauce over the noodles and vegetables. Toss continuously for 2-3 minutes until everything is well combined and heated through.

Adjust Seasoning:
- Taste and adjust the seasoning if needed. You can add more soy sauce or rice vinegar according to your taste.

Serve:
- Divide the Cabbage and Carrot Soba Noodle Stir-Fry among plates. Garnish with sesame seeds and serve with lime wedges on the side.

Enjoy this vibrant and flavorful stir-fry as a quick and wholesome meal!

Coconut Curry Shirataki Noodles

Ingredients:

For the Coconut Curry Sauce:

- 1 can (14 oz) coconut milk
- 2 tablespoons red curry paste
- 2 tablespoons soy sauce or tamari (for gluten-free)
- 1 tablespoon fish sauce
- 1 tablespoon coconut sugar or erythritol
- 1 tablespoon lime juice
- 1 teaspoon grated ginger
- 2 cloves garlic, minced

For the Stir-Fry:

- 2 packs (about 400g) shirataki noodles, drained and rinsed
- 2 tablespoons oil (vegetable or coconut oil)
- 1 onion, thinly sliced
- 1 bell pepper (color of your choice), thinly sliced
- 1 cup broccoli florets
- 1 cup snap peas, trimmed
- 1 cup tofu or protein of your choice, cubed
- Fresh cilantro and lime wedges for garnish

Instructions:

> Prepare Coconut Curry Sauce:
> - In a bowl, whisk together coconut milk, red curry paste, soy sauce, fish sauce, coconut sugar (or sweetener of choice), lime juice, grated ginger, and minced garlic. Set aside.
>
> Prepare Shirataki Noodles:
> - Rinse the shirataki noodles under cold water and drain them well. You may also want to blanch them in hot water for a couple of minutes to remove any residual odor.
>
> Stir-Fry Vegetables and Protein:
> - Heat oil in a large skillet or wok over medium-high heat. Add sliced onion and stir-fry for 2-3 minutes until softened.

- Add bell pepper, broccoli florets, snap peas, and cubed tofu (or your choice of protein). Stir-fry for an additional 5-7 minutes until the vegetables are tender-crisp and the tofu is lightly browned.

Add Shirataki Noodles:
- Add the prepared shirataki noodles to the skillet. Toss everything together until well combined.

Pour Coconut Curry Sauce:
- Pour the coconut curry sauce over the noodles and vegetables. Toss continuously for 3-5 minutes until everything is well coated and heated through.

Adjust Seasoning:
- Taste and adjust the seasoning if needed. You can add more soy sauce, lime juice, or red curry paste according to your taste.

Serve:
- Divide the Coconut Curry Shirataki Noodles among plates. Garnish with fresh cilantro and serve with lime wedges on the side.

Enjoy this flavorful and low-carb Coconut Curry Shirataki Noodles as a satisfying and comforting meal!

Spiralized Cucumber and Shrimp Salad

Ingredients:

For the Salad:

- 2 large cucumbers, spiralized
- 1 pound (about 450g) shrimp, peeled and deveined
- 1 cup cherry tomatoes, halved
- 1/2 red onion, thinly sliced
- 1/4 cup fresh cilantro, chopped
- 1/4 cup fresh mint, chopped
- 1/4 cup roasted peanuts, chopped (optional for garnish)

For the Dressing:

- 3 tablespoons fish sauce
- 2 tablespoons lime juice
- 1 tablespoon soy sauce or tamari (for gluten-free)
- 1 tablespoon rice vinegar
- 1 tablespoon sesame oil
- 1 tablespoon honey or maple syrup
- 1 clove garlic, minced
- 1 teaspoon grated ginger
- Red chili flakes to taste (optional)

Instructions:

Cook Shrimp:
- If shrimp is not already cooked, you can boil, steam, or sauté it until pink and opaque. Set aside to cool.

Prepare Dressing:
- In a small bowl, whisk together fish sauce, lime juice, soy sauce, rice vinegar, sesame oil, honey, minced garlic, grated ginger, and red chili flakes (if using). Adjust the seasoning to taste.

Assemble Salad:
- In a large bowl, combine spiralized cucumbers, cooked shrimp, cherry tomatoes, sliced red onion, chopped cilantro, and chopped mint.

Pour Dressing:
- Pour the dressing over the salad and toss everything together until well coated.

Chill:
- Place the salad in the refrigerator for at least 30 minutes to allow the flavors to meld and the salad to chill.

Garnish:
- Before serving, garnish with chopped roasted peanuts if desired.

Serve:
- Divide the Spiralized Cucumber and Shrimp Salad among plates. Serve chilled.

This salad is not only healthy but also bursting with fresh flavors. Enjoy it as a light meal or a refreshing side dish!

Almond Butter Thai Noodle Bowl

Ingredients:

For the Almond Butter Sauce:

- 1/3 cup almond butter
- 3 tablespoons soy sauce or tamari (for gluten-free)
- 2 tablespoons rice vinegar
- 1 tablespoon sesame oil
- 1 tablespoon honey or maple syrup
- 1 clove garlic, minced
- 1 teaspoon grated ginger
- 1 teaspoon Sriracha or chili sauce (adjust to taste)
- 2-3 tablespoons water (to thin the sauce)

For the Noodle Bowl:

- 8 oz (about 225g) rice noodles or soba noodles
- 2 tablespoons oil (vegetable or sesame oil)
- 1 bell pepper (color of your choice), thinly sliced
- 1 carrot, julienned
- 1 cup broccoli florets, blanched
- 1 cup snap peas, trimmed
- 1/4 cup fresh cilantro, chopped
- 1/4 cup chopped green onions
- Sesame seeds and chopped almonds for garnish

Optional Protein Additions:

- Grilled chicken, tofu, shrimp, or your choice of protein

Instructions:

    Prepare Almond Butter Sauce:
- In a bowl, whisk together almond butter, soy sauce, rice vinegar, sesame oil, honey, minced garlic, grated ginger, Sriracha, and water. Adjust the consistency by adding more water if needed.

    Cook Noodles:
- Cook the rice or soba noodles according to package instructions. Drain and rinse under cold water.

Stir-Fry Vegetables:
- Heat oil in a large skillet or wok over medium-high heat. Add sliced bell pepper, julienned carrot, blanched broccoli florets, and snap peas. Stir-fry for 5-7 minutes until the vegetables are tender-crisp.

Add Noodles:
- Add the cooked and drained noodles to the skillet with the stir-fried vegetables.

Pour Almond Butter Sauce:
- Pour the prepared almond butter sauce over the noodles and vegetables. Toss everything together until well coated.

Optional Protein:
- If adding protein, toss in grilled chicken, tofu, shrimp, or your choice of protein at this stage. Cook until the protein is heated through.

Garnish:
- Garnish the noodle bowl with chopped cilantro, green onions, sesame seeds, and chopped almonds.

Serve:
- Divide the Almond Butter Thai Noodle Bowl among bowls. Serve immediately and enjoy!

This noodle bowl is a flavorful combination of nutty almond butter, vibrant vegetables, and your choice of protein. It's a satisfying and easy-to-make dish for a delicious Thai-inspired meal.

Keto-friendly Miso Soup with Tofu Shirataki

Ingredients:

For the Miso Broth:

- 4 cups water
- 2 tablespoons miso paste (look for a low-carb miso paste or use white miso)
- 1 tablespoon soy sauce or tamari (for gluten-free)
- 1 tablespoon sesame oil
- 1 teaspoon grated ginger
- 1 clove garlic, minced
- 1 teaspoon rice vinegar
- Salt and pepper to taste

For the Soup:

- 2 packs (about 400g) tofu shirataki noodles, drained and rinsed
- 1/2 cup firm tofu, cubed
- 1 cup baby spinach or bok choy
- 2 green onions, sliced
- Nori sheets, sliced (optional for garnish)
- Sesame seeds (optional for garnish)

Instructions:

Prepare Tofu Shirataki Noodles:
- Rinse the tofu shirataki noodles under cold water and drain well. You may want to blanch them in hot water for a couple of minutes to remove any residual odor.

Make Miso Broth:
- In a pot, combine water, miso paste, soy sauce, sesame oil, grated ginger, minced garlic, rice vinegar, salt, and pepper. Whisk well and bring to a gentle simmer over medium heat. Be careful not to boil miso, as it can lose some of its flavor.

Add Tofu and Vegetables:
- Add cubed firm tofu to the miso broth. Allow it to simmer for a few minutes until the tofu is heated through.
- Add baby spinach or bok choy to the pot. Let it wilt in the hot broth.

Add Tofu Shirataki Noodles:

- Add the prepared tofu shirataki noodles to the pot. Stir gently to combine and heat through.

Adjust Seasoning:
- Taste the broth and adjust the seasoning if needed. You can add more soy sauce or salt according to your taste.

Serve:
- Divide the Miso Soup with Tofu Shirataki among bowls. Garnish with sliced green onions, nori sheets, and sesame seeds if desired.

This keto-friendly Miso Soup with Tofu Shirataki provides a comforting and flavorful alternative to traditional miso soup while keeping the carb count low. Enjoy this warm and nourishing soup as a satisfying meal!

Sesame Almond Zoodle Bowl

Ingredients:

For the Zoodles:

- 4 medium zucchinis, spiralized into noodles

For the Sesame Almond Sauce:

- 3 tablespoons almond butter
- 2 tablespoons soy sauce or tamari (for gluten-free)
- 1 tablespoon sesame oil
- 1 tablespoon rice vinegar
- 1 tablespoon water
- 1 teaspoon grated ginger
- 1 clove garlic, minced
- 1 teaspoon erythritol or your preferred sweetener
- Red chili flakes to taste (optional)

For the Bowl:

- 1 cup shredded cabbage
- 1 carrot, julienned
- 1 bell pepper (color of your choice), thinly sliced
- 1 cup broccoli florets, blanched
- 1/4 cup chopped green onions
- Sesame seeds for garnish
- Sliced almonds for garnish

Optional Protein Additions:

- Grilled chicken, tofu, shrimp, or your choice of protein

Instructions:

Prepare Zoodles:
- Spiralize the zucchinis into noodle shapes. Set aside.

Make Sesame Almond Sauce:
- In a bowl, whisk together almond butter, soy sauce, sesame oil, rice vinegar, water, grated ginger, minced garlic, sweetener, and red chili flakes (if using). Adjust the consistency with more water if needed.

Stir-Fry Zoodles:

- Heat a large skillet or wok over medium-high heat. Add the zucchini noodles and stir-fry for 2-3 minutes until they are slightly softened but still have a crunch.

Prepare Vegetables:
- In the same skillet, add shredded cabbage, julienned carrot, sliced bell pepper, and blanched broccoli florets. Stir-fry for an additional 3-5 minutes until the vegetables are tender-crisp.

Combine Zoodles and Vegetables:
- Add the stir-fried zucchini noodles to the skillet with the vegetables. Toss everything together until well combined.

Pour Sesame Almond Sauce:
- Pour the prepared sesame almond sauce over the zoodles and vegetables. Toss continuously for 2-3 minutes until everything is well coated and heated through.

Optional Protein:
- If adding protein, toss in grilled chicken, tofu, shrimp, or your choice of protein at this stage. Cook until the protein is heated through.

Garnish:
- Garnish the Sesame Almond Zoodle Bowl with chopped green onions, sesame seeds, and sliced almonds.

Serve:
- Divide the Sesame Almond Zoodle Bowl among plates. Serve immediately and enjoy!

This low-carb, sesame almond-flavored zoodle bowl is a tasty and satisfying alternative to traditional noodle bowls. Customize it with your favorite vegetables and protein for a wholesome meal!

Shirataki Noodle Tom Yum Soup

Ingredients:

For the Soup Base:

- 4 cups vegetable broth
- 2 stalks lemongrass, bruised and cut into 2-inch pieces
- 3 kaffir lime leaves, torn into pieces
- 1-2 red chili peppers, sliced (adjust to taste)
- 3 tablespoons lime juice
- 2 tablespoons fish sauce
- 1 tablespoon soy sauce or tamari (for gluten-free)
- 1 tablespoon erythritol or your preferred sweetener
- 1 tablespoon grated galangal or ginger
- 2 cloves garlic, minced

For the Shirataki Noodles and Vegetables:

- 2 packs (about 400g) shirataki noodles, drained and rinsed
- 1 cup mushrooms, sliced (shiitake or straw mushrooms work well)
- 1 medium tomato, cut into wedges
- 1/2 cup baby corn, halved
- 1/4 cup cilantro leaves, chopped
- 2 green onions, sliced
- Optional: Thai bird chilies for extra heat

Optional Protein Additions:

- Shrimp, tofu, or chicken, thinly sliced

Instructions:

Prepare Shirataki Noodles:
- Rinse the shirataki noodles under cold water and drain them well. If desired, you can blanch them in hot water for a couple of minutes to remove any residual odor.

Make the Soup Base:
- In a pot, combine vegetable broth, lemongrass, kaffir lime leaves, sliced red chili peppers, lime juice, fish sauce, soy sauce, sweetener, grated galangal (or ginger), and minced garlic. Bring to a simmer and let it cook for 10-15 minutes to infuse the flavors.

Add Vegetables and Protein:
- Add sliced mushrooms, tomato wedges, baby corn, and any optional protein (shrimp, tofu, or chicken) to the simmering soup. Cook until the vegetables are tender and the protein is cooked through.

Add Shirataki Noodles:
- Add the prepared shirataki noodles to the soup. Allow them to heat through for a few minutes.

Adjust Seasoning:
- Taste the soup and adjust the seasoning if needed. You can add more lime juice, fish sauce, or sweetener according to your taste.

Remove Lemongrass and Lime Leaves:
- Before serving, remove the lemongrass stalks and torn kaffir lime leaves from the soup.

Garnish:
- Garnish the Shirataki Noodle Tom Yum Soup with chopped cilantro, sliced green onions, and Thai bird chilies if you like it extra spicy.

Serve:
- Ladle the soup into bowls and serve hot.

Enjoy this low-carb, tangy, and aromatic Shirataki Noodle Tom Yum Soup as a satisfying and comforting Thai-inspired meal!

Jicama Pad Thai Salad

Ingredients:

For the Salad:

- 1 medium jicama, peeled and julienned
- 1 cup shredded carrots
- 1 cup bean sprouts
- 1 red bell pepper, thinly sliced
- 1 cucumber, julienned
- 1/2 cup chopped cilantro
- 1/4 cup chopped peanuts or cashews (for garnish)
- Lime wedges (for serving)

For the Pad Thai Sauce:

- 3 tablespoons soy sauce or tamari (for gluten-free)
- 2 tablespoons fish sauce
- 2 tablespoons rice vinegar
- 1 tablespoon lime juice
- 1 tablespoon sesame oil
- 1 tablespoon erythritol or your preferred sweetener
- 1 clove garlic, minced
- 1 teaspoon grated ginger
- Red chili flakes to taste (optional)

Optional Protein Additions:

- Grilled chicken, shrimp, or tofu

Instructions:

Prepare Jicama and Vegetables:
- Peel the jicama and julienne it into thin strips using a mandoline or a sharp knife.
- Shred carrots, thinly slice the red bell pepper, julienne the cucumber, and chop cilantro.

Make the Pad Thai Sauce:

- In a small bowl, whisk together soy sauce, fish sauce, rice vinegar, lime juice, sesame oil, sweetener, minced garlic, grated ginger, and red chili flakes (if using). Adjust the seasoning to taste.

Assemble the Salad:
- In a large bowl, combine jicama strips, shredded carrots, bean sprouts, sliced red bell pepper, julienned cucumber, and chopped cilantro.

Optional Protein:
- If adding protein, toss in grilled chicken, shrimp, or tofu at this stage.

Pour Pad Thai Sauce:
- Pour the prepared Pad Thai sauce over the salad. Toss everything together until well coated with the sauce.

Chill:
- Place the salad in the refrigerator for at least 30 minutes to allow the flavors to meld.

Garnish:
- Before serving, garnish the Jicama Pad Thai Salad with chopped peanuts or cashews.

Serve:
- Divide the salad among plates. Serve with lime wedges on the side.

Enjoy this vibrant and crunchy Jicama Pad Thai Salad as a refreshing and healthy meal!

Low-Carb Bibimbap Bowl

Ingredients:

For the Cauliflower Rice:

- 1 medium head of cauliflower, riced
- 1 tablespoon sesame oil
- Salt to taste

For the Bibimbap Toppings:

- 1 cup thinly sliced beef (ribeye or sirloin)
- 1 tablespoon soy sauce or tamari (for gluten-free)
- 1 tablespoon sesame oil
- 1 tablespoon erythritol or your preferred sweetener
- 1 tablespoon rice vinegar
- 2 cloves garlic, minced
- 1 teaspoon grated ginger
- 1 cup julienned carrots
- 1 cup spinach, blanched and squeezed dry
- 1 cup mung bean sprouts, blanched
- 1 cup shiitake mushrooms, sliced and sautéed
- 4 fried or poached eggs
- Kimchi for serving
- Sesame seeds and sliced green onions for garnish

Optional Gochujang Sauce:

- 2 tablespoons gochujang (Korean red pepper paste)
- 1 tablespoon soy sauce
- 1 tablespoon sesame oil
- 1 tablespoon water
- 1 teaspoon erythritol or your preferred sweetener

Instructions:

Prepare Cauliflower Rice:
- Rice the cauliflower using a food processor or box grater.
- In a large skillet, heat sesame oil over medium heat. Add the riced cauliflower and sauté for 5-7 minutes until tender. Season with salt to taste.

Marinate Beef:
- In a bowl, combine thinly sliced beef with soy sauce, sesame oil, sweetener, rice vinegar, minced garlic, and grated ginger. Let it marinate for at least 15-20 minutes.

Cook Bibimbap Toppings:
- In separate pans, cook the marinated beef, julienned carrots, blanched spinach, mung bean sprouts, and sautéed shiitake mushrooms. Set each ingredient aside.

Fry or Poach Eggs:
- Fry or poach the eggs according to your preference.

Make Gochujang Sauce (Optional):
- In a small bowl, whisk together gochujang, soy sauce, sesame oil, water, and sweetener to make the sauce.

Assemble Bibimbap Bowls:
- Divide the cauliflower rice among serving bowls.
- Arrange the marinated beef, julienned carrots, blanched spinach, mung bean sprouts, sautéed shiitake mushrooms, and fried or poached eggs on top of the cauliflower rice.

Garnish and Serve:
- Drizzle the optional gochujang sauce over the bowls.
- Garnish with sesame seeds and sliced green onions.
- Serve with kimchi on the side.

Enjoy this Low-Carb Bibimbap Bowl for a flavorful and satisfying meal that's perfect for those following a low-carb or keto lifestyle!

Egg Drop Shirataki Soup

Ingredients:

For the Soup Base:

- 4 cups chicken or vegetable broth
- 2 packs (about 400g) shirataki noodles, drained and rinsed
- 2 green onions, sliced
- 1 tablespoon soy sauce or tamari (for gluten-free)
- 1 teaspoon sesame oil
- 1/2 teaspoon grated ginger
- Salt and white pepper to taste

For the Egg Drop:

- 2 large eggs, beaten
- 1 tablespoon water
- 1 tablespoon soy sauce or tamari
- 1 teaspoon sesame oil
- Pinch of white pepper

Optional Additions:

- Sliced mushrooms
- Baby spinach
- Cooked shredded chicken or tofu
- Red pepper flakes for extra heat

Instructions:

Prepare Shirataki Noodles:
- Rinse the shirataki noodles under cold water and drain them well. If desired, you can blanch them in hot water for a couple of minutes to remove any residual odor.

Make the Soup Base:
- In a pot, bring the chicken or vegetable broth to a simmer. Add the drained shirataki noodles, sliced green onions, soy sauce, sesame oil, grated ginger, salt, and white pepper. Simmer for about 5-7 minutes.

Optional Additions:

- If you're adding extra ingredients like sliced mushrooms, baby spinach, or cooked shredded chicken/tofu, add them to the pot and let them cook until tender.

Prepare the Egg Mixture:
- In a bowl, whisk together beaten eggs, water, soy sauce, sesame oil, and a pinch of white pepper.

Create Egg Ribbons:
- Once the soup is simmering, stir it in a circular motion with a ladle. While stirring, slowly pour the egg mixture into the moving soup. The eggs will cook and create silky ribbons.

Adjust Seasoning:
- Taste the soup and adjust the seasoning if needed. You can add more soy sauce or salt according to your taste.

Serve:
- Ladle the Egg Drop Shirataki Soup into bowls. Garnish with additional sliced green onions and a dash of white pepper if desired.

Enjoy this light and satisfying Egg Drop Shirataki Soup as a low-carb and comforting meal!

Kelp Noodle Coconut Curry Bowl

Ingredients:

For the Coconut Curry Sauce:

- 1 can (14 oz) coconut milk
- 2 tablespoons red curry paste
- 2 tablespoons soy sauce or tamari (for gluten-free)
- 1 tablespoon fish sauce
- 1 tablespoon coconut sugar or erythritol
- 1 tablespoon lime juice
- 1 teaspoon grated ginger
- 2 cloves garlic, minced

For the Kelp Noodle Bowl:

- 2 packs (about 400g) kelp noodles, rinsed and drained
- 2 tablespoons coconut oil
- 1 onion, thinly sliced
- 1 bell pepper (color of your choice), thinly sliced
- 1 carrot, julienned
- 1 cup broccoli florets, blanched
- 1 cup snap peas, trimmed
- 1 cup tofu or protein of your choice, cubed
- Fresh cilantro and lime wedges for garnish

Instructions:

Prepare Kelp Noodles:
- Rinse the kelp noodles under cold water and drain them well. Set aside.

Make Coconut Curry Sauce:
- In a bowl, whisk together coconut milk, red curry paste, soy sauce, fish sauce, coconut sugar, lime juice, grated ginger, and minced garlic. Set aside.

Stir-Fry Vegetables and Tofu:
- In a large skillet or wok, heat coconut oil over medium-high heat. Add sliced onion, bell pepper, julienned carrot, and tofu (or protein of your choice). Stir-fry for 5-7 minutes until the vegetables are tender-crisp and the tofu is lightly browned.

Add Kelp Noodles:
- Add the prepared kelp noodles to the skillet. Toss everything together until well combined.

Pour Coconut Curry Sauce:
- Pour the coconut curry sauce over the noodles and vegetables. Toss continuously for 3-5 minutes until everything is well coated and heated through.

Adjust Seasoning:
- Taste and adjust the seasoning if needed. You can add more soy sauce or lime juice according to your taste.

Garnish:
- Garnish the Kelp Noodle Coconut Curry Bowl with fresh cilantro and serve with lime wedges on the side.

Serve:
- Divide the curry bowl among plates. Serve immediately and enjoy!

This Kelp Noodle Coconut Curry Bowl is a delicious and satisfying option for those looking to reduce their carb intake while still enjoying the flavors of a classic coconut curry dish.

Cabbage and Broccoli Lo Mein

Ingredients:

For the Lo Mein Sauce:

- 3 tablespoons soy sauce or tamari (for gluten-free)
- 2 tablespoons oyster sauce
- 1 tablespoon hoisin sauce
- 1 tablespoon sesame oil
- 1 tablespoon rice vinegar
- 1 tablespoon sweetener of your choice (honey, maple syrup, or brown sugar)
- 1 teaspoon grated ginger
- 2 cloves garlic, minced
- Red pepper flakes to taste (optional)

For the Lo Mein Stir-Fry:

- 8 oz (about 225g) lo mein or egg noodles
- 2 tablespoons oil (vegetable or sesame oil)
- 4 cups shredded cabbage
- 2 cups broccoli florets
- 1 carrot, julienned
- 3 green onions, sliced
- 1 cup sliced mushrooms (optional)
- Sesame seeds for garnish
- Chopped cilantro for garnish (optional)

Optional Protein Additions:

- Sliced chicken, beef, shrimp, or tofu

Instructions:

Cook Noodles:

- Cook the lo mein or egg noodles according to package instructions. Drain and set aside.

Prepare Lo Mein Sauce:

- In a bowl, whisk together soy sauce, oyster sauce, hoisin sauce, sesame oil, rice vinegar, sweetener, grated ginger, minced garlic, and red pepper flakes (if using).

Stir-Fry Vegetables:

- Heat oil in a large wok or skillet over medium-high heat. Add shredded cabbage, broccoli florets, julienned carrot, and sliced mushrooms (if using). Stir-fry for 5-7 minutes until the vegetables are tender-crisp.

Optional Protein:
- If adding protein, push the vegetables to the side of the wok and cook the protein until browned and cooked through. Then, mix it with the vegetables.

Combine with Noodles:
- Add the cooked noodles to the wok with the stir-fried vegetables. Toss everything together until the noodles are well-coated with the vegetables.

Pour Lo Mein Sauce:
- Pour the prepared lo mein sauce over the noodles and vegetables. Toss continuously for 2-3 minutes until everything is well combined and heated through.

Adjust Seasoning:
- Taste and adjust the seasoning if needed. You can add more soy sauce or sweetener according to your taste.

Garnish and Serve:
- Garnish the Cabbage and Broccoli Lo Mein with sliced green onions, sesame seeds, and chopped cilantro if desired.

Serve:
- Divide the lo mein among plates. Serve immediately and enjoy this flavorful and vegetable-packed stir-fry!

This Cabbage and Broccoli Lo Mein is a quick and satisfying dish that combines the goodness of crunchy vegetables with the savory flavors of a delicious sauce. Customize it with your favorite protein for a complete meal.

Peanut Zoodle Stir-Fry

Ingredients:

For the Peanut Sauce:

- 1/4 cup natural peanut butter
- 3 tablespoons soy sauce or tamari (for gluten-free)
- 2 tablespoons rice vinegar
- 1 tablespoon sesame oil
- 1 tablespoon sweetener of your choice (honey, maple syrup, or brown sugar)
- 1 teaspoon grated ginger
- 1 clove garlic, minced
- Red pepper flakes to taste (optional)
- Water to thin, as needed

For the Zoodle Stir-Fry:

- 4 medium zucchinis, spiralized into noodles (zoodles)
- 2 tablespoons oil (vegetable or sesame oil)
- 1 bell pepper (color of your choice), thinly sliced
- 1 carrot, julienned
- 1 cup broccoli florets
- 1 cup snap peas, trimmed
- 1 cup shredded cabbage
- 1/4 cup chopped green onions
- Sesame seeds and chopped peanuts for garnish

Optional Protein Additions:

- Grilled chicken, tofu, shrimp, or your choice of protein

Instructions:

Prepare Peanut Sauce:
- In a bowl, whisk together peanut butter, soy sauce, rice vinegar, sesame oil, sweetener, grated ginger, minced garlic, and red pepper flakes (if using). Add water gradually until you reach your desired consistency. Set aside.

Prepare Zoodles:
- Spiralize the zucchinis into noodle shapes using a spiralizer. Set aside.

Stir-Fry Vegetables:

- Heat oil in a large skillet or wok over medium-high heat. Add sliced bell pepper, julienned carrot, broccoli florets, snap peas, and shredded cabbage. Stir-fry for 5-7 minutes until the vegetables are tender-crisp.

Optional Protein:
- If adding protein, push the vegetables to the side of the skillet or wok and cook the protein until browned and cooked through. Then, mix it with the vegetables.

Add Zoodles:
- Add the spiralized zucchini noodles (zoodles) to the skillet. Toss everything together until the zoodles are just heated through, about 2-3 minutes.

Pour Peanut Sauce:
- Pour the prepared peanut sauce over the zoodles and vegetables. Toss continuously for 2-3 minutes until everything is well coated and heated through.

Adjust Seasoning:
- Taste and adjust the seasoning if needed. You can add more soy sauce or sweetener according to your taste.

Garnish and Serve:
- Garnish the Peanut Zoodle Stir-Fry with chopped green onions, sesame seeds, and chopped peanuts.

Serve:
- Divide the stir-fry among plates. Serve immediately and enjoy this delicious and healthy Peanut Zoodle Stir-Fry!

This Peanut Zoodle Stir-Fry is a delightful combination of crisp zoodles, colorful vegetables, and a rich peanut sauce. It's a perfect low-carb option that doesn't compromise on flavor!

Cucumber Soba Noodle Salad

Ingredients:

For the Soba Noodle Salad:

- 8 oz (about 225g) soba noodles
- 2 large cucumbers, julienned or spiralized
- 1 red bell pepper, thinly sliced
- 1 carrot, julienned
- 1/4 cup chopped cilantro
- 1/4 cup chopped mint leaves
- Sesame seeds for garnish
- Sliced green onions for garnish

For the Sesame Ginger Dressing:

- 3 tablespoons soy sauce or tamari (for gluten-free)
- 2 tablespoons rice vinegar
- 1 tablespoon sesame oil
- 1 tablespoon honey or maple syrup
- 1 tablespoon grated ginger
- 1 clove garlic, minced
- 1 teaspoon sesame seeds (optional)
- Red pepper flakes to taste (optional)

Instructions:

Cook Soba Noodles:
- Cook the soba noodles according to the package instructions. Drain and rinse under cold water to stop the cooking process. Set aside.

Prepare Vegetables:
- Julienne or spiralize the cucumbers, thinly slice the red bell pepper, and julienne the carrot. Place them in a large salad bowl.

Make Sesame Ginger Dressing:
- In a small bowl, whisk together soy sauce, rice vinegar, sesame oil, honey, grated ginger, minced garlic, sesame seeds (if using), and red pepper flakes (if using). Adjust the taste to your liking.

Assemble Salad:
- Add the cooked and cooled soba noodles to the bowl with the julienned vegetables.

- Pour the sesame ginger dressing over the noodles and vegetables.

Toss and Garnish:
- Gently toss everything together until the noodles and vegetables are well coated with the dressing.
- Garnish the salad with chopped cilantro, mint leaves, sesame seeds, and sliced green onions.

Chill (Optional):
- For enhanced flavor, you can refrigerate the salad for 30 minutes to allow the flavors to meld.

Serve:
- Divide the Cucumber Soba Noodle Salad into serving bowls. Serve chilled or at room temperature.

This Cucumber Soba Noodle Salad is a perfect blend of textures and flavors, making it a light and satisfying option for a quick lunch or dinner. Enjoy the refreshing taste of the vegetables and the savory sesame ginger dressing!

Tofu Shirataki Pad Kee Mao

Ingredients:

For the Tofu Shirataki Pad Kee Mao:

- 2 packs (about 400g) tofu shirataki noodles, drained and rinsed
- 2 tablespoons oil (vegetable or sesame oil)
- 1 block firm tofu, pressed and cubed
- 3 cloves garlic, minced
- 2 Thai bird chilies, sliced (adjust to taste)
- 1 bell pepper (color of your choice), thinly sliced
- 1 cup broccoli florets
- 1 carrot, julienned
- 1/2 cup Thai basil leaves (holy basil), if available
- 1/4 cup soy sauce or tamari (for gluten-free)
- 2 tablespoons oyster sauce
- 1 tablespoon fish sauce
- 1 tablespoon sweetener of your choice (honey, maple syrup, or brown sugar)
- 1 tablespoon rice vinegar
- Lime wedges for serving

Optional Garnish:

- Sliced green onions
- Bean sprouts
- Crushed peanuts
- Additional Thai bird chilies for extra heat

Instructions:

Prepare Tofu Shirataki Noodles:
- Rinse the tofu shirataki noodles under cold water and drain them well. If desired, you can blanch them in hot water for a couple of minutes to remove any residual odor.

Stir-Fry Tofu:
- Heat 1 tablespoon of oil in a large wok or skillet over medium-high heat. Add the cubed tofu and stir-fry until golden brown. Remove the tofu from the wok and set it aside.

Stir-Fry Vegetables:

- In the same wok, add another tablespoon of oil. Add minced garlic and sliced Thai bird chilies. Stir-fry for about 30 seconds until fragrant.
- Add bell pepper, broccoli florets, and julienned carrot to the wok. Stir-fry for 3-5 minutes until the vegetables are tender-crisp.

Add Tofu and Tofu Shirataki Noodles:
- Add the cooked tofu back to the wok. Add the prepared tofu shirataki noodles. Toss everything together until well combined.

Make Sauce:
- In a small bowl, whisk together soy sauce, oyster sauce, fish sauce, sweetener, and rice vinegar. Pour the sauce over the noodles and vegetables.

Add Thai Basil:
- Add Thai basil leaves to the wok. Toss until the basil wilts and the noodles are evenly coated with the sauce.

Adjust Seasoning:
- Taste and adjust the seasoning if needed. You can add more soy sauce, sweetener, or fish sauce according to your taste.

Serve:
- Divide the Tofu Shirataki Pad Kee Mao among plates. Garnish with sliced green onions, bean sprouts, crushed peanuts, and additional Thai bird chilies if desired. Serve with lime wedges on the side.

Enjoy this flavorful and low-carb Tofu Shirataki Pad Kee Mao as a spicy and satisfying Thai-inspired dish!

Keto Teriyaki Chicken Konjac Noodles

Ingredients:

For the Teriyaki Chicken:

- 1 lb (about 450g) boneless, skinless chicken thighs or breasts, thinly sliced
- 1/4 cup soy sauce or tamari (for gluten-free)
- 2 tablespoons sugar-free teriyaki sauce
- 1 tablespoon sesame oil
- 1 tablespoon rice vinegar
- 1 tablespoon sweetener of your choice (erythritol, monk fruit, or stevia)
- 2 cloves garlic, minced
- 1 teaspoon grated ginger
- 2 tablespoons cooking oil (vegetable or avocado oil)

For the Konjac Noodles:

- 2 packs (about 400g) konjac noodles, drained and rinsed

Optional Garnish:

- Sesame seeds
- Sliced green onions
- Red pepper flakes for heat
- Steamed broccoli or vegetables of your choice

Instructions:

Prepare Teriyaki Chicken:
- In a bowl, combine soy sauce, sugar-free teriyaki sauce, sesame oil, rice vinegar, sweetener, minced garlic, and grated ginger to make the teriyaki marinade.
- Add sliced chicken to the marinade and let it marinate for at least 15-20 minutes.

Cook Chicken:
- Heat cooking oil in a skillet or wok over medium-high heat. Add the marinated chicken and cook until browned and cooked through, about 5-7 minutes.

Prepare Konjac Noodles:

- Rinse the konjac noodles under cold water and drain them well. If desired, you can blanch them in hot water for a couple of minutes to remove any residual odor.

Combine Chicken and Noodles:
- Add the prepared konjac noodles to the skillet with the cooked chicken. Toss everything together until the noodles are well-coated with the teriyaki sauce.

Adjust Seasoning:
- Taste and adjust the seasoning if needed. You can add more soy sauce, teriyaki sauce, or sweetener according to your taste.

Optional Steamed Vegetables:
- If desired, you can steam broccoli or your favorite vegetables separately and add them to the skillet with the chicken and noodles.

Garnish:
- Garnish the Keto Teriyaki Chicken with konjac noodles with sesame seeds, sliced green onions, and red pepper flakes for extra heat.

Serve:
- Divide the dish among plates. Serve immediately and enjoy this keto-friendly and low-carb Teriyaki Chicken with Konjac Noodles!

This Keto Teriyaki Chicken with Konjac Noodles is a satisfying and flavorful dish that allows you to enjoy the classic teriyaki flavors while keeping it low-carb. Customize it with your favorite keto-friendly vegetables for a complete meal!

Lemongrass Chicken Shirataki Bowl

Ingredients:

For the Lemongrass Chicken:

- 1 lb (about 450g) boneless, skinless chicken thighs or breasts, thinly sliced
- 2 tablespoons soy sauce or tamari (for gluten-free)
- 2 tablespoons fish sauce
- 1 tablespoon sweetener of your choice (honey, maple syrup, or erythritol)
- 2 stalks lemongrass, outer layers removed and finely minced
- 2 cloves garlic, minced
- 1 tablespoon grated ginger
- 1 tablespoon sesame oil
- 2 tablespoons cooking oil (vegetable or avocado oil)

For the Shirataki Bowl:

- 2 packs (about 400g) shirataki noodles, drained and rinsed
- 1 cup shredded cabbage
- 1 carrot, julienned
- 1 bell pepper (color of your choice), thinly sliced
- 1/4 cup chopped cilantro
- 1/4 cup chopped mint leaves
- Lime wedges for serving

Optional Garnish:

- Sliced green onions
- Crushed peanuts
- Red pepper flakes for heat

Instructions:

Prepare Lemongrass Chicken:
- In a bowl, combine soy sauce, fish sauce, sweetener, minced lemongrass, minced garlic, grated ginger, and sesame oil to create the marinade.
- Add sliced chicken to the marinade and let it marinate for at least 15-20 minutes.

Cook Lemongrass Chicken:

- Heat cooking oil in a skillet or wok over medium-high heat. Add the marinated chicken and cook until browned and cooked through, about 5-7 minutes.

Prepare Shirataki Noodles:
- Rinse the shirataki noodles under cold water and drain them well. If desired, you can blanch them in hot water for a couple of minutes to remove any residual odor.

Stir-Fry Vegetables:
- In the same skillet or wok, add shredded cabbage, julienned carrot, and sliced bell pepper. Stir-fry for 3-5 minutes until the vegetables are tender-crisp.

Combine Chicken and Noodles:
- Add the cooked lemongrass chicken to the skillet with the stir-fried vegetables. Toss everything together until well combined.

Assemble the Bowl:
- Divide the shirataki noodles among serving bowls. Top with the lemongrass chicken and stir-fried vegetables.

Garnish:
- Garnish the Lemongrass Chicken Shirataki Bowl with chopped cilantro, mint leaves, and optional sliced green onions, crushed peanuts, and red pepper flakes.

Serve:
- Serve the bowls with lime wedges on the side. Squeeze lime juice over the bowl before eating.

Enjoy this Lemongrass Chicken Shirataki Bowl as a light, fragrant, and low-carb meal with a perfect balance of flavors!

Radish Noodle Kimchi Bibim Guksu

Ingredients:

For the Radish Noodle Kimchi Bibim Guksu:

- 2 packs (about 400g) radish noodles (or use spiralized daikon radish)
- 1 cup kimchi, chopped
- 1/4 cup gochujang (Korean red pepper paste)
- 2 tablespoons soy sauce or tamari (for gluten-free)
- 1 tablespoon sesame oil
- 1 tablespoon rice vinegar
- 1 tablespoon sweetener of your choice (honey, maple syrup, or brown sugar)
- 1 tablespoon toasted sesame seeds
- 1 cucumber, julienned
- 1 carrot, julienned
- 2 green onions, sliced
- Fresh cilantro and/or mint leaves for garnish

Optional Protein Additions:

- Hard-boiled eggs, sliced
- Grilled chicken, beef, or tofu

Instructions:

Prepare Radish Noodles:
- If using radish noodles, rinse them under cold water and drain well. If using spiralized daikon radish, blanch the noodles in hot water for 2-3 minutes. Drain and let them cool.

Make Bibim Guksu Sauce:
- In a bowl, whisk together gochujang, soy sauce, sesame oil, rice vinegar, sweetener, and toasted sesame seeds to create the bibim guksu sauce.

Assemble Bibim Guksu:
- In a large mixing bowl, combine the radish noodles, chopped kimchi, julienned cucumber, julienned carrot, and sliced green onions.

Add Sauce:
- Pour the bibim guksu sauce over the noodles and vegetables. Toss everything together until well coated with the sauce.

Optional Protein:

- If adding protein, top the bibim guksu with sliced hard-boiled eggs, grilled chicken, beef, or tofu.

Chill (Optional):
- For enhanced flavor, you can refrigerate the bibim guksu for 30 minutes to allow the flavors to meld.

Garnish:
- Garnish the Radish Noodle Kimchi Bibim Guksu with fresh cilantro and/or mint leaves.

Serve:
- Divide the bibim guksu among serving bowls. Serve immediately and enjoy this spicy and refreshing Korean cold noodle dish!

This Radish Noodle Kimchi Bibim Guksu is a perfect dish for hot days or when you crave a flavorful and spicy meal. Customize it with your preferred protein for a complete and satisfying experience!

Thai Basil Zoodle Bowl

Ingredients:

For the Thai Basil Sauce:

- 1/4 cup soy sauce or tamari (for gluten-free)
- 2 tablespoons fish sauce
- 1 tablespoon oyster sauce
- 1 tablespoon sweetener of your choice (honey, maple syrup, or brown sugar)
- 1 tablespoon lime juice
- 1 tablespoon rice vinegar
- 1 tablespoon sesame oil
- 1 Thai bird chili, finely chopped (adjust to taste)
- 2 cloves garlic, minced

For the Zoodle Bowl:

- 4 medium zucchinis, spiralized into noodles (zoodles)
- 2 tablespoons oil (vegetable or sesame oil)
- 1 lb (about 450g) shrimp, chicken, or tofu, cooked and seasoned
- 1 bell pepper (color of your choice), thinly sliced
- 1 carrot, julienned
- 1 cup snap peas, trimmed
- 1/4 cup fresh Thai basil leaves
- Crushed peanuts and lime wedges for garnish

Instructions:

Prepare Thai Basil Sauce:
- In a bowl, whisk together soy sauce, fish sauce, oyster sauce, sweetener, lime juice, rice vinegar, sesame oil, chopped Thai bird chili, and minced garlic. Set aside.

Cook Protein:
- Cook and season your choice of protein (shrimp, chicken, or tofu) according to your preference. Set aside.

Stir-Fry Vegetables:
- Heat oil in a large wok or skillet over medium-high heat. Add sliced bell pepper, julienned carrot, and snap peas. Stir-fry for 3-5 minutes until the vegetables are tender-crisp.

Add Zoodles:

- Add the spiralized zucchini noodles (zoodles) to the wok. Toss everything together until the zoodles are just heated through, about 2-3 minutes.

Pour Thai Basil Sauce:
- Pour the prepared Thai Basil Sauce over the zoodles and vegetables. Toss continuously for 2-3 minutes until everything is well combined and heated through.

Assemble the Bowl:
- Divide the zoodle mixture among serving bowls. Top with the cooked and seasoned protein of your choice.

Garnish:
- Garnish the Thai Basil Zoodle Bowl with fresh Thai basil leaves, crushed peanuts, and lime wedges.

Serve:
- Serve the bowls immediately, allowing everyone to squeeze lime juice over their bowls before eating.

Enjoy this Thai Basil Zoodle Bowl for a light, flavorful, and low-carb meal that's quick to prepare and bursting with Thai-inspired goodness!

Low-Carb Ramen with Chicken and Bok Choy

Ingredients:

For the Broth:

- 4 cups chicken broth (homemade or store-bought, preferably low-sodium)
- 2 tablespoons soy sauce or tamari (for gluten-free)
- 1 tablespoon sesame oil
- 1 tablespoon rice vinegar
- 1 tablespoon grated ginger
- 2 cloves garlic, minced
- 1 teaspoon chili garlic sauce (adjust to taste)
- Salt and pepper to taste

For the Ramen Bowl:

- 2 packs (about 400g) shirataki noodles or spiralized zucchini noodles
- 1 lb (about 450g) boneless, skinless chicken thighs or breasts, thinly sliced
- 4 baby bok choy, halved
- 2 green onions, sliced
- Sesame seeds for garnish
- Soft-boiled eggs, halved (optional)

Optional Toppings:

- Sliced mushrooms
- Bean sprouts
- Red chili flakes for heat
- Nori seaweed strips

Instructions:

Prepare the Broth:
- In a pot, combine chicken broth, soy sauce, sesame oil, rice vinegar, grated ginger, minced garlic, and chili garlic sauce. Bring the mixture to a simmer and let it cook for about 10-15 minutes to allow the flavors to meld. Season with salt and pepper to taste.

Prepare the Chicken:
- Season the thinly sliced chicken with salt and pepper. In a separate skillet, cook the chicken in a bit of oil over medium-high heat until browned and cooked through.

Prepare the Bok Choy:
- Steam or blanch the baby bok choy halves for 2-3 minutes until they are tender-crisp. Set aside.

Prepare the Noodles:
- If using shirataki noodles, rinse them under cold water and drain well. If using spiralized zucchini noodles, you can blanch them for 1-2 minutes in hot water to soften slightly.

Assemble the Ramen Bowl:
- Divide the noodles among serving bowls. Top with the cooked chicken, steamed bok choy, and sliced green onions.

Pour the Broth:
- Ladle the hot broth over the noodles, chicken, and vegetables in each bowl.

Garnish:
- Garnish the Low-Carb Ramen with sesame seeds and optional toppings like sliced mushrooms, bean sprouts, red chili flakes, and nori seaweed strips.

Optional Soft-Boiled Eggs:
- If desired, add soft-boiled eggs to each bowl.

Serve:
- Serve the Low-Carb Ramen with Chicken and Bok Choy immediately and enjoy this comforting and low-carb alternative to traditional ramen!

Feel free to customize this recipe with your favorite low-carb vegetables and protein options for a bowl of ramen that suits your taste preferences.

Cabbage Pad Thai Salad

Ingredients:

For the Dressing:

- 1/4 cup soy sauce or tamari (for gluten-free)
- 2 tablespoons fish sauce
- 2 tablespoons rice vinegar
- 1 tablespoon lime juice
- 1 tablespoon sweetener of your choice (honey, maple syrup, or brown sugar)
- 1 tablespoon sesame oil
- 1 teaspoon grated ginger
- 1 clove garlic, minced
- 1 teaspoon chili garlic sauce (adjust to taste)

For the Salad:

- 1 small green cabbage, thinly shredded
- 1 carrot, julienned
- 1 red bell pepper, thinly sliced
- 1 cup bean sprouts
- 1/2 cup chopped cilantro
- 1/4 cup chopped peanuts
- Lime wedges for serving

Optional Protein Additions:

- Grilled chicken, shrimp, tofu, or your choice of protein

Instructions:

Prepare the Dressing:
- In a bowl, whisk together soy sauce, fish sauce, rice vinegar, lime juice, sweetener, sesame oil, grated ginger, minced garlic, and chili garlic sauce. Set aside.

Assemble the Salad:
- In a large mixing bowl, combine shredded cabbage, julienned carrot, sliced red bell pepper, bean sprouts, and chopped cilantro.

Add the Dressing:

- Pour the dressing over the salad. Toss everything together until the vegetables are well coated with the dressing.

Optional Protein:
- If adding protein, top the salad with grilled chicken, shrimp, tofu, or your choice of protein.

Garnish:
- Garnish the Cabbage Pad Thai Salad with chopped peanuts.

Serve:
- Divide the salad among serving plates. Serve with lime wedges on the side for squeezing over the salad before eating.

Enjoy this Cabbage Pad Thai Salad as a light and vibrant dish that captures the essence of traditional Pad Thai in a refreshing salad form. Customize it with your preferred protein for a complete and satisfying meal!

Spaghetti Squash Bulgogi Bowl

Ingredients:

For the Bulgogi Marinade:

- 1 lb (about 450g) beef sirloin or ribeye, thinly sliced
- 1/4 cup soy sauce or tamari (for gluten-free)
- 2 tablespoons brown sugar or sweetener of your choice
- 1 tablespoon sesame oil
- 1 tablespoon mirin or rice wine
- 1 tablespoon grated pear or apple
- 2 cloves garlic, minced
- 1 teaspoon grated ginger
- 1 tablespoon sesame seeds
- 2 green onions, sliced
- Black pepper to taste

For the Spaghetti Squash:

- 1 medium-sized spaghetti squash
- 1 tablespoon olive oil
- Salt and pepper to taste

For the Bowl:

- Sautéed or steamed vegetables of your choice (bell peppers, carrots, broccoli, etc.)
- Sesame seeds for garnish
- Sliced green onions for garnish
- Kimchi (optional)
- Cooked rice or cauliflower rice (optional, for a low-carb version)

Instructions:

Prepare the Spaghetti Squash:
- Preheat the oven to 400°F (200°C).
- Cut the spaghetti squash in half lengthwise. Scoop out the seeds.
- Rub the cut sides of the squash with olive oil and season with salt and pepper.
- Place the squash halves, cut side down, on a baking sheet.

- Roast in the oven for 40-50 minutes or until the flesh is tender and can be easily shredded with a fork.
- Use a fork to scrape the spaghetti-like strands from the squash.

Prepare the Bulgogi Marinade:
- In a bowl, whisk together soy sauce, brown sugar, sesame oil, mirin, grated pear or apple, minced garlic, grated ginger, sesame seeds, sliced green onions, and black pepper.
- Add the thinly sliced beef to the marinade. Allow it to marinate for at least 30 minutes, or ideally, refrigerate for a few hours or overnight for better flavor.

Cook Bulgogi:
- Heat a skillet or wok over medium-high heat.
- Add the marinated beef and cook for 3-5 minutes until the meat is browned and cooked through.

Sauté Vegetables:
- In the same skillet, sauté or steam your choice of vegetables until they are tender-crisp.

Assemble the Bowl:
- Divide the spaghetti squash strands among serving bowls.
- Top with the cooked bulgogi and sautéed vegetables.

Garnish:
- Garnish the Spaghetti Squash Bulgogi Bowl with sesame seeds and sliced green onions.
- Add kimchi on the side for extra flavor and a spicy kick.

Serve:
- Serve the bowls immediately, optionally over cooked rice or cauliflower rice for a low-carb version.

Enjoy this Spaghetti Squash Bulgogi Bowl as a satisfying and flavorful meal that combines the goodness of marinated beef, spaghetti squash, and a variety of vegetables!

Keto-friendly Pho with Kelp Noodles

Ingredients:

For the Broth:

- 8 cups beef or vegetable broth (homemade or store-bought, preferably low-sodium)
- 1 onion, halved and unpeeled
- 1 3-inch piece of ginger, sliced
- 2-3 star anise
- 2-3 whole cloves
- 1 cinnamon stick
- 1 cardamom pod
- 1 tablespoon fish sauce
- Salt and pepper to taste

For the Pho Bowl:

- 2 packs (about 400g) kelp noodles, rinsed and drained
- 1 lb (about 450g) thinly sliced beef (sirloin or flank)
- 1 cup bean sprouts
- Fresh herbs (cilantro, basil, mint)
- Sliced green onions
- Lime wedges
- Jalapeño slices (optional)
- Sriracha or hot sauce (optional)

Instructions:

Prepare the Broth:
- In a large pot, char the onion and ginger over an open flame or under the broiler until they are slightly blackened. This enhances the flavor of the broth.
- In the same pot, add the charred onion and ginger, star anise, cloves, cinnamon stick, cardamom pod, fish sauce, and beef or vegetable broth.
- Bring the broth to a boil, then reduce the heat to low and simmer for at least 30 minutes to allow the flavors to meld.
- Season the broth with salt and pepper to taste.

Prepare Kelp Noodles:

- Rinse the kelp noodles under cold water and drain them well.

Sear the Beef:
- Arrange the thinly sliced beef on a plate. Pour a small amount of hot broth over the beef to quickly cook and slightly sear it. Set aside.

Assemble the Pho Bowl:
- Divide the kelp noodles among serving bowls.
- Top the noodles with the seared beef slices.

Strain and Pour Broth:
- Strain the broth to remove the solid ingredients, and then pour the hot broth over the kelp noodles and beef.

Garnish:
- Add bean sprouts, fresh herbs (cilantro, basil, mint), sliced green onions, and jalapeño slices if desired.

Serve:
- Serve the Keto-friendly Pho with lime wedges and offer Sriracha or hot sauce on the side for those who prefer more heat.

Enjoy this Keto-friendly Pho with Kelp Noodles as a satisfying and comforting meal that stays true to the authentic Pho flavors while keeping the carbs in check.

Shirataki Noodle Teriyaki Salmon Bowl

Ingredients:

For the Teriyaki Salmon:

- 2 salmon fillets
- 1/4 cup soy sauce or tamari (for gluten-free)
- 2 tablespoons mirin
- 1 tablespoon sake or dry white wine
- 1 tablespoon sweetener of your choice (honey, maple syrup, or brown sugar)
- 1 tablespoon sesame oil
- 1 teaspoon grated ginger
- 2 cloves garlic, minced
- 1 green onion, sliced (for garnish)

For the Shirataki Noodles:

- 2 packs (about 400g) shirataki noodles, drained and rinsed
- 1 tablespoon sesame oil
- 1 cup broccoli florets
- 1 carrot, julienned
- 1 bell pepper (color of your choice), thinly sliced
- 1/4 cup soy sauce or tamari (for gluten-free)

Optional Toppings:

- Sesame seeds
- Sliced green onions
- Red pepper flakes for heat
- Avocado slices

Instructions:

Prepare the Teriyaki Salmon:
- In a bowl, whisk together soy sauce, mirin, sake or white wine, sweetener, sesame oil, grated ginger, and minced garlic to create the teriyaki marinade.
- Place the salmon fillets in a shallow dish and pour half of the teriyaki marinade over them. Let them marinate for at least 15-20 minutes.

Cook the Teriyaki Salmon:

- Preheat the oven to 400°F (200°C).
- Place the marinated salmon fillets on a baking sheet lined with parchment paper.
- Bake for 12-15 minutes or until the salmon is cooked through and flakes easily.
- While the salmon is baking, heat the remaining teriyaki marinade in a small saucepan over medium heat. Simmer until it thickens into a glaze.

Prepare Shirataki Noodles:
- Heat sesame oil in a skillet or wok over medium-high heat.
- Add broccoli florets, julienned carrot, and thinly sliced bell pepper. Stir-fry for 3-5 minutes until the vegetables are tender-crisp.
- Add shirataki noodles to the skillet and pour soy sauce over them. Toss everything together until well combined and heated through.

Assemble the Bowl:
- Divide the shirataki noodle and vegetable mixture among serving bowls.
- Top with the teriyaki salmon fillets.

Drizzle with Teriyaki Glaze:
- Drizzle the thickened teriyaki glaze over the salmon fillets.

Garnish:
- Garnish the Shirataki Noodle Teriyaki Salmon Bowl with sliced green onions, sesame seeds, and red pepper flakes if desired.
- Optionally, add avocado slices for extra creaminess.

Serve:
- Serve the bowls immediately, and enjoy this low-carb and flavorful Teriyaki Salmon Bowl!

This Shirataki Noodle Teriyaki Salmon Bowl is a delightful combination of tender teriyaki salmon and low-carb shirataki noodles, creating a satisfying and healthy meal.

Sesame Ginger Cabbage Noodles

Ingredients:

For the Sesame Ginger Sauce:

- 3 tablespoons soy sauce or tamari (for gluten-free)
- 1 tablespoon sesame oil
- 1 tablespoon rice vinegar
- 1 tablespoon sweetener of your choice (honey, maple syrup, or brown sugar)
- 1 tablespoon grated ginger
- 2 cloves garlic, minced
- 1 teaspoon sesame seeds
- Red pepper flakes for heat (optional)

For the Cabbage Noodles:

- 1 small green cabbage, thinly sliced or shredded
- 2 tablespoons oil (vegetable or sesame oil)
- 2 green onions, sliced (for garnish)
- 1 tablespoon sesame seeds (for garnish)

Optional Protein Additions:

- Grilled chicken, shrimp, tofu, or your choice of protein

Instructions:

Prepare Sesame Ginger Sauce:
- In a small bowl, whisk together soy sauce, sesame oil, rice vinegar, sweetener, grated ginger, minced garlic, sesame seeds, and red pepper flakes if using. Set aside.

Prepare Cabbage Noodles:
- Heat oil in a large skillet or wok over medium-high heat.
- Add the thinly sliced or shredded cabbage to the skillet. Stir-fry for 5-7 minutes until the cabbage is tender-crisp.

Add Sesame Ginger Sauce:
- Pour the prepared Sesame Ginger Sauce over the cabbage noodles. Toss everything together until the cabbage is well coated with the sauce.

Optional Protein:

- If adding protein, such as grilled chicken, shrimp, or tofu, add it to the skillet and toss until heated through and well combined with the cabbage noodles.

Garnish:
- Garnish the Sesame Ginger Cabbage Noodles with sliced green onions and sesame seeds.

Serve:
- Divide the cabbage noodles among serving plates. Serve immediately, and enjoy this low-carb and flavorful dish!

This Sesame Ginger Cabbage Noodles recipe provides a satisfying crunch and a burst of Asian-inspired flavors without the carb-heavy noodles. Feel free to customize it with your favorite protein or additional vegetables for a complete and wholesome meal.

Almond Butter Chicken Zoodle Stir-Fry

Ingredients:

For the Almond Butter Sauce:

- 1/4 cup almond butter
- 3 tablespoons soy sauce or tamari (for gluten-free)
- 2 tablespoons rice vinegar
- 1 tablespoon sesame oil
- 1 tablespoon sweetener of your choice (honey, maple syrup, or brown sugar)
- 1 tablespoon grated ginger
- 2 cloves garlic, minced
- Red pepper flakes for heat (optional)
- Water to thin, if needed

For the Chicken Zoodle Stir-Fry:

- 1 lb (about 450g) boneless, skinless chicken breasts, thinly sliced
- 4 medium zucchinis, spiralized into noodles (zoodles)
- 2 tablespoons oil (vegetable or sesame oil)
- 1 bell pepper (color of your choice), thinly sliced
- 1 carrot, julienned
- 1 cup broccoli florets
- Green onions, sliced, for garnish
- Sesame seeds, for garnish

Optional Toppings:

- Crushed peanuts
- Cilantro leaves
- Lime wedges

Instructions:

Prepare Almond Butter Sauce:
- In a bowl, whisk together almond butter, soy sauce, rice vinegar, sesame oil, sweetener, grated ginger, minced garlic, and red pepper flakes if using. If the sauce is too thick, you can thin it with a bit of water.

Stir-Fry Chicken:
- In a large skillet or wok, heat oil over medium-high heat.

- Add the thinly sliced chicken and stir-fry until browned and cooked through, about 5-7 minutes.

Add Vegetables:
- Add the spiralized zucchini, sliced bell pepper, julienned carrot, and broccoli florets to the skillet. Stir-fry for an additional 3-5 minutes until the vegetables are tender-crisp.

Combine with Almond Butter Sauce:
- Pour the prepared Almond Butter Sauce over the chicken and vegetables in the skillet. Toss everything together until well coated with the sauce.

Garnish:
- Garnish the Almond Butter Chicken Zoodle Stir-Fry with sliced green onions and sesame seeds.

Optional Toppings:
- If desired, top with crushed peanuts, cilantro leaves, and serve with lime wedges on the side.

Serve:
- Divide the stir-fry among serving plates. Serve immediately and enjoy this flavorful and low-carb Almond Butter Chicken Zoodle Stir-Fry!

This recipe offers a delightful combination of protein-packed chicken, crisp vegetables, and a creamy almond butter sauce over zucchini noodles, providing a satisfying and nutritious meal.

Jicama Noodle Spring Roll Bowl

Ingredients:

For the Peanut Lime Sauce:

- 1/4 cup peanut butter
- 3 tablespoons soy sauce or tamari (for gluten-free)
- 2 tablespoons lime juice
- 1 tablespoon rice vinegar
- 1 tablespoon sweetener of your choice (honey, maple syrup, or brown sugar)
- 1 teaspoon sesame oil
- 1 clove garlic, minced
- 1 teaspoon grated ginger
- Red pepper flakes for heat (optional)
- Water to thin, if needed

For the Jicama Noodle Spring Roll Bowl:

- 1 medium-sized jicama, peeled and spiralized into noodles
- 1 cup shredded red cabbage
- 1 carrot, julienned
- 1 cucumber, julienned
- 1 bell pepper (color of your choice), thinly sliced
- 1 cup bean sprouts
- Fresh mint leaves
- Fresh cilantro leaves
- Roasted peanuts, chopped, for garnish
- Sesame seeds, for garnish

Optional Protein Additions:

- Grilled shrimp, chicken, tofu, or your choice of protein

Instructions:

Prepare Peanut Lime Sauce:
- In a bowl, whisk together peanut butter, soy sauce, lime juice, rice vinegar, sweetener, sesame oil, minced garlic, grated ginger, and red pepper flakes if using. If the sauce is too thick, you can thin it with a bit of water.

Prepare Jicama Noodles:
- Peel the jicama and spiralize it into noodles using a spiralizer.

Assemble the Bowl:
- In a large mixing bowl, combine the jicama noodles, shredded red cabbage, julienned carrot, julienned cucumber, sliced bell pepper, and bean sprouts.

Add Peanut Lime Sauce:
- Pour the Peanut Lime Sauce over the vegetables. Toss everything together until well coated with the sauce.

Optional Protein:
- If adding protein, such as grilled shrimp, chicken, tofu, or your choice of protein, add it to the bowl and toss to combine.

Garnish:
- Garnish the Jicama Noodle Spring Roll Bowl with fresh mint leaves, cilantro leaves, chopped roasted peanuts, and sesame seeds.

Serve:
- Divide the spring roll bowl among serving plates. Serve immediately and enjoy this light and crunchy Jicama Noodle Spring Roll Bowl!

This recipe provides a burst of freshness and vibrant flavors, making it a perfect option for a light and healthy meal. Customize it with your preferred protein for added satisfaction.

Spiralized Daikon Radish Yakisoba

Ingredients:

For the Yakisoba Sauce:

- 1/4 cup soy sauce or tamari (for gluten-free)
- 2 tablespoons Worcestershire sauce
- 1 tablespoon oyster sauce
- 1 tablespoon sweetener of your choice (honey, maple syrup, or brown sugar)
- 1 tablespoon sake or dry white wine
- 1 teaspoon sesame oil
- 1 clove garlic, minced
- 1 teaspoon grated ginger

For the Spiralized Daikon Radish Yakisoba:

- 2 large daikon radishes, peeled and spiralized into noodles
- 2 tablespoons oil (vegetable or sesame oil)
- 1 onion, thinly sliced
- 1 carrot, julienned
- 1 bell pepper (color of your choice), thinly sliced
- 2 cups shredded cabbage
- 1 cup bean sprouts
- 1 cup sliced mushrooms
- Green onions, sliced, for garnish
- Sesame seeds, for garnish

Optional Protein Additions:

- Thinly sliced chicken, beef, shrimp, tofu, or your choice of protein

Instructions:

Prepare Yakisoba Sauce:
- In a bowl, whisk together soy sauce, Worcestershire sauce, oyster sauce, sweetener, sake or white wine, sesame oil, minced garlic, and grated ginger. Set aside.

Spiralize Daikon Radish:
- Peel the daikon radishes and spiralize them into noodle-like strands using a spiralizer.

Stir-Fry Vegetables:

- Heat oil in a large skillet or wok over medium-high heat.
- Add sliced onion, julienned carrot, sliced bell pepper, shredded cabbage, bean sprouts, and sliced mushrooms to the skillet. Stir-fry for 5-7 minutes until the vegetables are tender-crisp.

Add Spiralized Daikon Radish:
- Add the spiralized daikon radish noodles to the skillet. Toss everything together and stir-fry for an additional 3-5 minutes until the daikon noodles are just tender.

Pour Yakisoba Sauce:
- Pour the prepared Yakisoba Sauce over the vegetables and daikon noodles. Toss everything together until well coated with the sauce.

Optional Protein:
- If adding protein, such as thinly sliced chicken, beef, shrimp, tofu, or your choice of protein, add it to the skillet and stir-fry until cooked through.

Garnish:
- Garnish the Spiralized Daikon Radish Yakisoba with sliced green onions and sesame seeds.

Serve:
- Divide the yakisoba among serving plates. Serve immediately and enjoy this low-carb and flavorful Spiralized Daikon Radish Yakisoba!

This recipe offers a satisfying and healthy twist on the classic yakisoba, providing a delicious alternative to traditional wheat noodles. Feel free to customize it with your preferred protein for added variety.

Cauliflower Kimchi Fried Rice Bowl

Ingredients:

For the Kimchi Fried Rice:

- 1 medium-sized cauliflower, grated or processed into rice-sized pieces
- 1 cup kimchi, chopped
- 2 tablespoons oil (vegetable or sesame oil)
- 2 green onions, sliced
- 2 cloves garlic, minced
- 1 tablespoon soy sauce or tamari (for gluten-free)
- 1 tablespoon oyster sauce
- 1 teaspoon sesame oil
- 1/2 cup frozen peas and carrots, thawed
- 2 eggs, beaten
- Salt and pepper to taste

Optional Toppings:

- Sliced green onions
- Sesame seeds
- Fried egg on top

Optional Protein Additions:

- Diced tofu, cooked chicken, shrimp, or your choice of protein

Instructions:

Prepare Cauliflower Rice:
- Grate the cauliflower using a box grater or process it in a food processor until it resembles rice-sized pieces.

Stir-Fry Vegetables:
- Heat oil in a large skillet or wok over medium-high heat.
- Add sliced green onions and minced garlic to the skillet. Stir-fry for 1-2 minutes until fragrant.

Add Cauliflower Rice:
- Add the grated cauliflower to the skillet. Stir-fry for 5-7 minutes until the cauliflower is cooked and slightly golden.

Add Kimchi and Seasonings:

- Add chopped kimchi, soy sauce, oyster sauce, and sesame oil to the cauliflower rice. Stir everything together until well combined.

Stir in Peas and Carrots:
- Add the thawed frozen peas and carrots to the skillet. Stir-fry for an additional 2-3 minutes until they are heated through.

Create Well in the Center:
- Push the cauliflower rice and vegetables to the sides of the skillet, creating a well in the center.

Scramble Eggs:
- Pour the beaten eggs into the well in the center. Allow them to set for a moment, and then scramble them until cooked.

Combine Everything:
- Mix the scrambled eggs with the cauliflower rice and vegetables until well combined.

Season and Garnish:
- Season the Cauliflower Kimchi Fried Rice with salt and pepper to taste. Garnish with sliced green onions and sesame seeds.

Optional Toppings:
- For an extra touch, top the fried rice with a fried egg.

Serve:
- Divide the cauliflower kimchi fried rice among serving bowls. Serve immediately and enjoy this low-carb and flavorful dish!

Feel free to customize this recipe by adding your choice of protein or other favorite vegetables to suit your taste preferences.

Zoodle Tom Kha Gai Soup

Ingredients:

For the Tom Kha Gai Broth:

- 4 cups chicken broth
- 1 can (13.5 oz) coconut milk
- 2 lemongrass stalks, bruised and cut into 2-inch pieces
- 3-4 kaffir lime leaves
- 1 inch galangal or ginger, sliced
- 2-3 Thai bird chilies, sliced (adjust to taste)
- 2 tablespoons fish sauce
- 1 tablespoon soy sauce or tamari (for gluten-free)
- 1 tablespoon lime juice
- 1 tablespoon coconut sugar or sweetener of your choice
- Salt to taste

For the Zoodle Tom Kha Gai Soup:

- 2 medium zucchinis, spiralized into noodles (zoodles)
- 1 cup cooked chicken, shredded
- 1 cup mushrooms, sliced
- 1 medium tomato, diced
- 1 small onion, thinly sliced
- 2 cloves garlic, minced
- Cilantro leaves, for garnish
- Thai basil leaves, for garnish
- Sliced red chilies, for garnish (optional)
- Lime wedges, for serving

Instructions:

Prepare the Tom Kha Gai Broth:
- In a pot, combine chicken broth, coconut milk, lemongrass, kaffir lime leaves, galangal or ginger, sliced Thai bird chilies, fish sauce, soy sauce, lime juice, and coconut sugar.
- Bring the mixture to a simmer over medium heat. Allow it to simmer for about 15-20 minutes to infuse the flavors.
- Season the broth with salt to taste.

Sauté Vegetables:
- In a separate skillet, heat a bit of oil over medium heat.
- Add sliced onions, minced garlic, mushrooms, and diced tomatoes to the skillet. Sauté until the vegetables are softened.

Add Zoodles and Chicken:
- Add the zucchini noodles (zoodles) and shredded cooked chicken to the skillet. Sauté for an additional 2-3 minutes until the zoodles are just tender.

Strain and Combine:
- Strain the Tom Kha Gai broth to remove the solid ingredients, and then pour the hot broth over the zoodles, chicken, and vegetables in the skillet.

Garnish and Serve:
- Garnish the Zoodle Tom Kha Gai Soup with cilantro leaves, Thai basil leaves, and sliced red chilies if using.
- Serve the soup immediately with lime wedges on the side.

Enjoy:
- Enjoy this low-carb and flavorful Zoodle Tom Kha Gai Soup as a light and comforting meal!

This recipe provides a delicious and low-carb alternative to the traditional Tom Kha Gai soup, incorporating zucchini noodles for added freshness and texture. Adjust the level of spiciness and sweetness according to your taste preferences.

Cabbage and Shrimp Soba Noodle Stir-Fry

Ingredients:

For the Stir-Fry Sauce:

- 3 tablespoons soy sauce or tamari (for gluten-free)
- 1 tablespoon oyster sauce
- 1 tablespoon hoisin sauce
- 1 tablespoon rice vinegar
- 1 tablespoon sweetener of your choice (honey, maple syrup, or brown sugar)
- 1 teaspoon sesame oil
- 1 teaspoon grated ginger
- 2 cloves garlic, minced
- Red pepper flakes for heat (optional)

For the Cabbage and Shrimp Soba Noodle Stir-Fry:

- 8 oz (about 225g) soba noodles
- 2 tablespoons oil (vegetable or sesame oil)
- 1 lb (about 450g) large shrimp, peeled and deveined
- 4 cups shredded cabbage
- 1 carrot, julienned
- 1 bell pepper (color of your choice), thinly sliced
- 2 green onions, sliced
- Sesame seeds for garnish
- Fresh cilantro for garnish (optional)
- Lime wedges for serving

Instructions:

Prepare the Stir-Fry Sauce:
- In a bowl, whisk together soy sauce, oyster sauce, hoisin sauce, rice vinegar, sweetener, sesame oil, grated ginger, minced garlic, and red pepper flakes if using. Set aside.

Cook Soba Noodles:
- Cook the soba noodles according to the package instructions. Drain and rinse them under cold water to stop the cooking process. Set aside.

Sauté Shrimp:
- Heat oil in a large skillet or wok over medium-high heat.

- Add the shrimp and cook for 2-3 minutes on each side until they are pink and opaque. Remove shrimp from the skillet and set aside.

Sauté Vegetables:
- In the same skillet, add a bit more oil if needed.
- Add shredded cabbage, julienned carrot, and sliced bell pepper to the skillet. Stir-fry for 3-4 minutes until the vegetables are tender-crisp.

Combine with Noodles and Sauce:
- Add the cooked and drained soba noodles to the skillet.
- Pour the prepared stir-fry sauce over the noodles and vegetables. Toss everything together until well combined.

Add Shrimp:
- Return the cooked shrimp to the skillet. Toss to incorporate with the noodles and vegetables.

Garnish:
- Garnish the Cabbage and Shrimp Soba Noodle Stir-Fry with sliced green onions, sesame seeds, and fresh cilantro if using.

Serve:
- Divide the stir-fry among serving plates. Serve immediately with lime wedges on the side.

Enjoy this Cabbage and Shrimp Soba Noodle Stir-Fry as a flavorful and wholesome meal that combines the goodness of soba noodles, shrimp, and a variety of colorful vegetables!

Keto-friendly Laksa with Shirataki Noodles

Ingredients:

For the Laksa Broth:

- 2 tablespoons coconut oil
- 1 onion, finely chopped
- 2 cloves garlic, minced
- 1 tablespoon ginger, grated
- 2 tablespoons Laksa paste (store-bought or homemade)
- 4 cups chicken or vegetable broth
- 1 can (14 oz) coconut milk
- 1 tablespoon fish sauce
- 1 tablespoon soy sauce or tamari (for gluten-free)
- 1 teaspoon curry powder
- 1 teaspoon chili paste (adjust to taste)
- Salt and pepper to taste

For the Laksa Bowl:

- 2 packs (about 400g) shirataki noodles, rinsed and drained
- 1 cup cooked chicken, shredded
- 1 cup shrimp, peeled and deveined
- Bean sprouts
- Fresh cilantro leaves
- Lime wedges

Optional Toppings:

- Hard-boiled eggs, halved
- Sliced green onions
- Fried tofu cubes

Instructions:

Prepare Laksa Broth:
- In a large pot, heat coconut oil over medium heat. Add chopped onion, minced garlic, and grated ginger. Sauté until the onion is translucent.

Add Laksa Paste:
- Stir in Laksa paste and cook for 2-3 minutes until fragrant.

Pour Broth:

- Pour in chicken or vegetable broth and bring the mixture to a simmer.

Season Broth:
- Add coconut milk, fish sauce, soy sauce, curry powder, and chili paste. Season with salt and pepper to taste. Simmer for 15-20 minutes to allow flavors to meld.

Prepare Shirataki Noodles:
- Rinse and drain shirataki noodles. You can briefly boil them or pan-fry them to improve the texture.

Cook Chicken and Shrimp:
- In a separate pan, cook shredded chicken and shrimp until they are cooked through.

Assemble the Laksa Bowl:
- Divide the shirataki noodles among serving bowls.
- Top with cooked chicken, shrimp, and bean sprouts.

Pour Laksa Broth:
- Ladle the hot Laksa broth over the noodles and toppings.

Garnish:
- Garnish the Keto-friendly Laksa with fresh cilantro leaves and lime wedges.
- Add optional toppings such as hard-boiled eggs, sliced green onions, or fried tofu cubes.

Serve:
- Serve the Keto-friendly Laksa immediately, and enjoy the rich and aromatic flavors without the carbs!

Feel free to customize this Keto-friendly Laksa with your favorite low-carb ingredients and adjust the spice level according to your preference. It's a satisfying and flavorful alternative to the traditional noodle soup.

Thai Basil Beef and Cucumber Noodles

Ingredients:

For the Thai Basil Beef:

- 1 lb (about 450g) lean ground beef
- 2 tablespoons oil (vegetable or sesame oil)
- 4 cloves garlic, minced
- 1 red chili, thinly sliced (adjust to taste)
- 1 cup fresh Thai basil leaves

For the Cucumber Noodles:

- 2 large cucumbers, spiralized into noodles
- 1 carrot, julienned
- 1 red bell pepper, thinly sliced
- 1/2 cup cherry tomatoes, halved

For the Sauce:

- 3 tablespoons soy sauce or tamari (for gluten-free)
- 1 tablespoon fish sauce
- 1 tablespoon oyster sauce
- 1 tablespoon sweetener of your choice (honey, maple syrup, or brown sugar)
- 1 tablespoon lime juice

Optional Garnishes:

- Sliced green onions
- Crushed peanuts
- Red pepper flakes for extra heat

Instructions:

   Prepare the Thai Basil Beef:
   - In a large skillet or wok, heat oil over medium-high heat.
   - Add minced garlic and sliced red chili. Sauté for about 30 seconds until fragrant.
   - Add ground beef and cook until browned, breaking it apart with a spoon as it cooks.

- Once the beef is cooked, stir in Thai basil leaves and cook for an additional minute until the basil is wilted. Remove from heat and set aside.

Prepare the Cucumber Noodles:
- Spiralize the cucumbers into noodle-like strands.
- In a large mixing bowl, combine cucumber noodles, julienned carrot, sliced red bell pepper, and cherry tomatoes.

Prepare the Sauce:
- In a small bowl, whisk together soy sauce, fish sauce, oyster sauce, sweetener, and lime juice to create the sauce.

Assemble the Dish:
- Pour the sauce over the cucumber noodles and toss to coat the vegetables evenly.

Top with Thai Basil Beef:
- Arrange the Thai Basil Beef on top of the cucumber noodles.

Garnish:
- Garnish the dish with sliced green onions, crushed peanuts, and red pepper flakes if desired.

Serve:
- Serve the Thai Basil Beef and Cucumber Noodles immediately, and enjoy the fresh and bold flavors of this low-carb Thai-inspired dish!

Feel free to customize this recipe based on your preferences, adding more vegetables or adjusting the level of spiciness. It's a quick and flavorful option for a light and satisfying meal.

Kelp Noodle Thai Coconut Soup

Ingredients:

For the Thai Coconut Soup Base:

- 4 cups chicken or vegetable broth
- 1 can (14 oz) coconut milk
- 2 lemongrass stalks, bruised and cut into 2-inch pieces
- 3-4 kaffir lime leaves
- 1 inch galangal or ginger, sliced
- 2-3 Thai bird chilies, sliced (adjust to taste)
- 2 tablespoons fish sauce
- 1 tablespoon soy sauce or tamari (for gluten-free)
- 1 tablespoon lime juice
- 1 tablespoon coconut sugar or sweetener of your choice
- Salt to taste

For the Kelp Noodle Thai Coconut Soup:

- 2 packs (about 400g) kelp noodles, rinsed and drained
- 1 cup sliced mushrooms
- 1 cup baby bok choy, chopped
- 1 cup cherry tomatoes, halved
- 1 cup cooked chicken, shredded (optional)
- Fresh cilantro leaves for garnish
- Lime wedges for serving

Optional Toppings:

- Sliced green onions
- Thai basil leaves
- Red chili flakes for extra heat

Instructions:

Prepare the Thai Coconut Soup Base:
- In a pot, combine chicken or vegetable broth, coconut milk, lemongrass, kaffir lime leaves, galangal or ginger, sliced Thai bird chilies, fish sauce, soy sauce, lime juice, and coconut sugar.

- Bring the mixture to a simmer over medium heat. Allow it to simmer for about 15-20 minutes to infuse the flavors.
- Season the broth with salt to taste.

Prepare Kelp Noodles:
- Rinse and drain kelp noodles. You can briefly boil them or pan-fry them to improve the texture.

Add Vegetables and Chicken:
- Add sliced mushrooms, chopped baby bok choy, cherry tomatoes, and shredded cooked chicken (if using) to the simmering broth. Cook for an additional 5-7 minutes until the vegetables are tender.

Add Kelp Noodles:
- Add the prepared kelp noodles to the soup. Stir to combine and heat through.

Garnish and Serve:
- Garnish the Kelp Noodle Thai Coconut Soup with fresh cilantro leaves and lime wedges.
- Optionally, top with sliced green onions, Thai basil leaves, and red chili flakes for added flavor.

Serve:
- Ladle the hot soup into serving bowls. Serve immediately and enjoy this low-carb and flavorful Kelp Noodle Thai Coconut Soup!

Feel free to adjust the spice level and customize the soup with your favorite vegetables. It's a comforting and nutritious option for those seeking a low-carb alternative to traditional noodle soups.

Spiralized Zucchini and Chicken Satay Bowl

Ingredients:

For the Chicken Satay:

- 1 lb (about 450g) boneless, skinless chicken breasts, cut into thin strips
- 1/4 cup peanut butter
- 2 tablespoons soy sauce or tamari (for gluten-free)
- 1 tablespoon lime juice
- 1 tablespoon sesame oil
- 1 tablespoon sweetener of your choice (honey, maple syrup, or brown sugar)
- 1 clove garlic, minced
- 1 teaspoon grated ginger
- 1 teaspoon curry powder
- Wooden skewers, soaked in water

For the Spiralized Zucchini Bowl:

- 4 medium zucchinis, spiralized into noodles
- 1 cup shredded carrots
- 1 red bell pepper, thinly sliced
- 1 cup bean sprouts
- 1/4 cup chopped peanuts for garnish
- Fresh cilantro leaves for garnish

Optional Dressing:

- Additional peanut sauce or a simple lime vinaigrette

Instructions:

Prepare Chicken Satay:
- In a bowl, whisk together peanut butter, soy sauce, lime juice, sesame oil, sweetener, minced garlic, grated ginger, and curry powder to create the satay marinade.
- Thread chicken strips onto soaked wooden skewers and coat them with the satay marinade. Allow the chicken to marinate for at least 30 minutes.

Cook Chicken Satay:
- Grill or pan-cook the chicken skewers until fully cooked, about 5-7 minutes per side.

Prepare Spiralized Zucchini Bowl:

- Spiralize the zucchinis into noodle-like strands.
- In a large bowl, combine spiralized zucchinis, shredded carrots, sliced red bell pepper, and bean sprouts.

Assemble the Bowl:
- Arrange the spiralized zucchini and vegetable mixture in serving bowls.

Top with Chicken Satay:
- Remove the cooked chicken from the skewers and place them on top of the spiralized vegetables.

Garnish:
- Garnish the bowl with chopped peanuts and fresh cilantro leaves.

Optional Dressing:
- Drizzle additional peanut sauce or a simple lime vinaigrette over the bowl if desired.

Serve:
- Serve the Spiralized Zucchini and Chicken Satay Bowl immediately and enjoy this flavorful and low-carb meal!

Feel free to customize this recipe by adding more vegetables or adjusting the level of spice in the satay marinade. It's a satisfying and healthy alternative that captures the essence of chicken satay in a vegetable-packed bowl.

Teriyaki Tofu Shirataki Noodle Bowl

Ingredients:

For the Teriyaki Tofu:

- 1 block (14 oz) firm tofu, pressed and cubed
- 2 tablespoons soy sauce or tamari (for gluten-free)
- 2 tablespoons mirin
- 1 tablespoon sake or rice vinegar
- 1 tablespoon sweetener of your choice (honey, maple syrup, or brown sugar)
- 1 teaspoon sesame oil
- 1 tablespoon cornstarch (optional, for extra crispiness)
- 2 tablespoons oil for cooking

For the Shirataki Noodle Bowl:

- 2 packs (about 400g) tofu shirataki noodles, rinsed and drained
- 1 cup broccoli florets, blanched
- 1 carrot, julienned
- 1 red bell pepper, thinly sliced
- 2 green onions, sliced
- Sesame seeds for garnish
- Chopped cilantro for garnish (optional)

For the Teriyaki Sauce:

- 3 tablespoons soy sauce or tamari (for gluten-free)
- 2 tablespoons mirin
- 1 tablespoon sake or rice vinegar
- 1 tablespoon sweetener of your choice (honey, maple syrup, or brown sugar)
- 1 teaspoon sesame oil
- 1 clove garlic, minced
- 1 teaspoon grated ginger
- 1 tablespoon cornstarch mixed with 2 tablespoons water (for thickening)

Instructions:

    Prepare Teriyaki Tofu:
- In a bowl, whisk together soy sauce, mirin, sake or rice vinegar, sweetener, and sesame oil to create the teriyaki marinade.

- Add the cubed tofu to the marinade and let it marinate for at least 15-30 minutes.
- If desired, toss the marinated tofu in cornstarch for extra crispiness.
- In a pan, heat oil over medium-high heat. Add the marinated tofu and cook until golden and crispy on all sides. Set aside.

Prepare Teriyaki Sauce:
- In a small saucepan, combine soy sauce, mirin, sake or rice vinegar, sweetener, sesame oil, minced garlic, and grated ginger. Bring to a simmer.
- Add the cornstarch-water mixture to the sauce and cook, stirring continuously, until the sauce thickens. Remove from heat.

Prepare Shirataki Noodle Bowl:
- Rinse and drain tofu shirataki noodles. You can briefly boil them or pan-fry them to improve the texture.
- In a large bowl, combine the shirataki noodles with blanched broccoli, julienned carrot, sliced red bell pepper, and sliced green onions.

Assemble the Bowl:
- Arrange the shirataki noodle and vegetable mixture in serving bowls.
- Top with the crispy teriyaki tofu.

Pour Teriyaki Sauce:
- Drizzle the prepared teriyaki sauce over the bowl.

Garnish:
- Garnish the Teriyaki Tofu Shirataki Noodle Bowl with sesame seeds and chopped cilantro if desired.

Serve:
- Serve the bowl immediately and enjoy this delicious and low-carb Teriyaki Tofu Shirataki Noodle dish!

Feel free to customize this recipe by adding more vegetables or adjusting the level of sweetness and spiciness in the teriyaki sauce. It's a flavorful and satisfying option for a low-carb meal.

Cucumber and Radish Somen Salad

Ingredients:

For the Salad:

- 8 oz (about 225g) somen noodles, cooked according to package instructions, and cooled
- 1 cucumber, julienned
- 1 bunch radishes, thinly sliced
- 1/4 cup chopped fresh cilantro
- 1/4 cup chopped fresh mint
- 1/4 cup chopped roasted peanuts

For the Dressing:

- 3 tablespoons rice vinegar
- 2 tablespoons soy sauce or tamari (for gluten-free)
- 1 tablespoon sesame oil
- 1 tablespoon honey or sweetener of your choice
- 1 teaspoon grated ginger
- 1 clove garlic, minced
- Red pepper flakes (optional, for heat)

Instructions:

Prepare the Somen Noodles:
- Cook the somen noodles according to the package instructions. Once cooked, rinse them under cold water and set aside to cool.

Prepare the Dressing:
- In a small bowl, whisk together rice vinegar, soy sauce, sesame oil, honey, grated ginger, minced garlic, and red pepper flakes if using. Set aside.

Assemble the Salad:
- In a large bowl, combine the cooked and cooled somen noodles with julienned cucumber, thinly sliced radishes, chopped cilantro, and chopped mint.

Toss with Dressing:
- Pour the dressing over the noodle and vegetable mixture. Toss everything together until well coated with the dressing.

Chill (Optional):

- If desired, chill the salad in the refrigerator for about 30 minutes before serving to enhance the flavors.

Garnish:
- Garnish the salad with chopped roasted peanuts just before serving.

Serve:
- Serve the Cucumber and Radish Somen Salad in individual bowls. Enjoy the light and refreshing flavors!

Feel free to customize this salad by adding other fresh vegetables or herbs that you enjoy. The combination of somen noodles, crisp vegetables, and the flavorful dressing makes it a perfect dish for a quick and satisfying meal.

Low-Carb Vietnamese Bun Thit Nuong Bowl

Ingredients:

For the Grilled Pork:

- 1 lb (about 450g) pork shoulder or pork loin, thinly sliced
- 3 tablespoons soy sauce or tamari (for gluten-free)
- 2 tablespoons fish sauce
- 1 tablespoon sugar substitute (erythritol, monk fruit, or your choice)
- 1 tablespoon vegetable oil
- 2 cloves garlic, minced
- 1 teaspoon sesame oil
- 1 teaspoon lemongrass paste (or finely minced fresh lemongrass)
- 1/2 teaspoon black pepper

For the Nuoc Cham Sauce (Dipping Sauce):

- 3 tablespoons fish sauce
- 2 tablespoons rice vinegar
- 1 tablespoon sugar substitute
- 1/2 cup water
- 1 clove garlic, minced
- 1 red chili, thinly sliced (optional)

For the Low-Carb Bun Thit Nuong Bowl:

- 1 head of lettuce (butter lettuce or iceberg lettuce works well), leaves separated
- 1 cucumber, julienned
- 1 carrot, julienned
- Bean sprouts
- Fresh herbs (mint, cilantro, and basil)
- Crushed peanuts for garnish

Instructions:

Marinate and Grill the Pork:
- In a bowl, mix together soy sauce, fish sauce, sugar substitute, vegetable oil, minced garlic, sesame oil, lemongrass paste, and black pepper.
- Add thinly sliced pork to the marinade and let it marinate for at least 30 minutes.

- Grill the marinated pork slices until cooked and slightly charred on the edges.

Prepare Nuoc Cham Sauce:
- In a bowl, whisk together fish sauce, rice vinegar, sugar substitute, water, minced garlic, and sliced red chili if using. Adjust the taste to your liking.

Assemble the Low-Carb Bun Thit Nuong Bowl:
- On a plate, arrange lettuce leaves as the base.
- Top with grilled pork slices, julienned cucumber, julienned carrot, bean sprouts, and fresh herbs.

Drizzle with Nuoc Cham Sauce:
- Drizzle the assembled bowl with the prepared Nuoc Cham sauce.

Garnish:
- Garnish the Low-Carb Bun Thit Nuong Bowl with crushed peanuts.

Serve:
- Serve immediately, and enjoy this low-carb and refreshing version of Bun Thit Nuong!

Feel free to customize your bowl by adding other low-carb vegetables or herbs that you enjoy. This dish is a flavorful and satisfying option for those looking to reduce their carb intake while still enjoying the vibrant flavors of Vietnamese cuisine.

Cauliflower Shrimp Pad See Ew

Ingredients:

For the Cauliflower "Rice" Noodles:

- 1 large cauliflower head, grated or processed into rice-like texture
- 2 tablespoons oil for stir-frying

For the Shrimp Pad See Ew:

- 1 lb (about 450g) large shrimp, peeled and deveined
- 2 tablespoons soy sauce or tamari (for gluten-free)
- 1 tablespoon oyster sauce
- 1 tablespoon fish sauce
- 1 tablespoon sweetener of your choice (honey, maple syrup, or brown sugar)
- 2 tablespoons vegetable oil for stir-frying
- 3 cloves garlic, minced
- 2 eggs, lightly beaten
- 2 cups Chinese broccoli or broccoli florets
- 1 cup carrot, julienned
- 2 green onions, sliced
- Crushed red pepper flakes (optional, for heat)

Optional Garnish:

- Fresh cilantro leaves
- Lime wedges

Instructions:

Prepare Cauliflower "Rice" Noodles:
- Grate the cauliflower head or process it in a food processor until it resembles rice. Set aside.

Marinate Shrimp:
- In a bowl, combine shrimp with soy sauce, oyster sauce, fish sauce, and sweetener. Allow them to marinate for about 15-20 minutes.

Stir-Fry Shrimp:
- Heat 2 tablespoons of vegetable oil in a large wok or skillet over medium-high heat.
- Add minced garlic and stir-fry for 30 seconds until fragrant.

- Add the marinated shrimp and cook until they turn pink and opaque. Remove them from the wok and set aside.

Stir-Fry Vegetables:
- In the same wok, add a bit more oil if needed.
- Add julienned carrots and Chinese broccoli (or broccoli florets). Stir-fry until the vegetables are tender-crisp.

Push Vegetables to the Side:
- Push the vegetables to one side of the wok and pour the beaten eggs into the other side. Scramble the eggs until cooked through.

Combine Ingredients:
- Add the grated cauliflower "rice" to the wok. Stir-fry to combine all the ingredients.

Add Shrimp and Sauce:
- Return the cooked shrimp to the wok.
- Pour the sauce over the entire mixture and toss everything together until well-coated.

Finish Cooking:
- Stir in sliced green onions and cook for an additional 1-2 minutes until everything is heated through.
- If desired, add crushed red pepper flakes for extra heat.

Garnish and Serve:
- Garnish the Cauliflower Shrimp Pad See Ew with fresh cilantro leaves and serve with lime wedges on the side.

Enjoy:
- Serve immediately and enjoy this low-carb and flavorful Cauliflower Shrimp Pad See Ew!

Feel free to adjust the vegetables and spice levels according to your preference. This dish offers a tasty and healthier twist on the classic Pad See Ew with the use of cauliflower "rice."

www.ingramcontent.com/pod-product-compliance
Lightning Source LLC
LaVergne TN
LVHW081600060526
838201LV00054B/1998